The Ethics of Management

LaRue Tone Hosmer
Graduate School of Business Administration
University of Michigan

Third Edition

IRWIN

Chicago • Bogotá • Boston • Buenos Aires • Caracas
London • Madrid • Mexico City • Sydney • Toronto

Irwin Book Team

Sponsoring editor: *John E. Biernat*
Editorial assistant: *Kimberly Kanakes*
Marketing manager: *Michael Campbell*
Project Editor: *Rebecca Dodson*
Production supervisor: *Laurie Kersch*
Manager, graphics and desktop services: *Kim Meriwether*
Designer: *Crispin Prebys*
Cover Designer: *Crispin Prebys*
Compositor: *Douglas & Gayle, Ltd*
Typeface: *10.5/12 Times Roman*
Printer: *Quebecor Book Group*

TIMES MIRROR
HIGHER EDUCATION GROUP

Library of Congress Cataloging-in-Publication Data

Hosmer, LaRue T.
    The ethics of management / LaRue Tone Hosmer.—3rd ed.
    p. cm.
    Includes index.
    ISBN 0-256-12797-2
    1. Business ethics.   2. Industrial management—Moral and ethical
aspects.   I. Title.
HF5387.H67 1996
174'.4—dc20   95—34922

Printed in the United States of America
1 2 3 4 5 6 7 8 9 0 Q 2 1 0 9 8 7 6 5

Preface

What is "right" and "proper" and "just"? These terms, and that question, are going to become more important in the future than in the past as our society becomes more crowded, our economy more competitive, and our technology more complex. These terms and that question are going to become particularly important for the business executive, whose decisions can affect so many people in ways that are outside of their own control.

The ethics of management—the determination of what is "right" and "proper" and "just" in the decisions and actions that affect other people—goes far beyond simple questions of bribery, theft, and collusion. It focuses on what our relationships are—and ought to be—with our employees, our customers, our stockholders, our creditors, our suppliers, our distributors, and neighbors—members of the communities in which we operate. What do we owe to an employee who has been with the company for 28 years, yet now is no longer needed? What do we owe to a customer who purchased one of our mechanical products 3 years ago, yet now we realize that it may fail in operation and cause that person great inconvenience, and perhaps some loss of safety? What do we owe to distributor who helped us establish a major product line years ago, yet now represents an inefficient means of reaching the market? What do we owe to our stockholders, and how do we balance our duties to our stockholders with our obligations to these other groups?

This is the most critical issue in the ethics of management: the continual conflict between the economic performance of the firm, measured by revenues, costs, and profits and owed to the stockholders, and the social performance of the firm, much more difficult to measure, but represented by obligations to employees, customers, creditors, suppliers, distributors, and members of the general public. If we discharge our employee who has 28 years of service but is no longer needed, our costs will go down yet his life may be ruined. If we don't tell our customer about the design flaw in our product, our warranty expenses will be lower yet she may be seriously inconvenienced and perhaps even hurt. If we replace our distributor by shipping directly from the factory to the retailers, our profits will increase yet we may force that company out of business.

How do we decide when we face these issues? How do we determine what is "right" and "proper" and "just" in these and other instances?

This book looks at how we decide. It first considers the nature of the moral dilemma in business—this conflict between economic and social performance. Moral dilemmas in management are not simple choices between "right" and "wrong"; they are complex judgments on the balance between economic returns and social damages, complicated by the multiple alternatives, extended consequences, uncertain probabilities, and career implications that are an inherent part of these decisions.

The book then examines three alternative means of arriving at a decision when faced with an ethical conflict:

1. Economic analysis, relying on impersonal market forces.

2. Legal analysis, relying on impersonal social rules.

3. Ethical analysis, relying on personal moral values and ethical principles.

None of these means of analysis are satisfactory by themselves. But, all together they do form a means of moral reasoning that can help a manager to arrive at a decision that he or she can feel to be "right" and "proper" and "just." The book makes no effort to dictate what is "right" and "proper" and "just;" instead that is left to the individual's own moral standards of behavior and ethical systems of belief. The intent is to provide an understanding, for individuals, of the reasoning process that makes use of these moral standards of behavior and ethical systems of belief so that each individual can form his/her reasoned judgment when faced with a business decision that is, by the very nature of the decision, going to injure someone else.

Lastly, let me say that I am not the only person to have thought about the question of what is "right" and "proper" and "just" in management. There are lots of other theorists and practioners. I have learned greatly from both groups, and should like to acknowledge my debt to Richard DeGeorge (Kansas), Manuel Velasquez (Santa Clara), Thomas Donaldson (Georgetown), Patricia Werhane (Virginia), Gerald Cavanagh (Detroit), William Fredrick (Pittsburgh), Edwin Epstein (Berkeley), Oliver Williams (Notre Dame), Lisa Newton (Fairfield), Kirk Hanson (Stanford), and Nicholas Steneck (Michigan). I thank you all.

Contents

Strategic Causes of the Accident. Written Code of Ethics to Convey Performance Expectations. Informal Review Process to Advise on Performance Expectations. Reexamination of the Strategy, Structure, Systems, and Style. The Moral Responsibilities of Senior Management.

CHAPTER 1

The Nature of Ethics in Management

Ethical issues occur frequently in management. They extend far beyond the commonly discussed problems of bribery, collusion, and theft, reaching into such areas as corporate acquisitions, marketing policies, and capital investments. A large corporation has taken over a smaller one through the common practice of negotiating for the purchase of stock. Then, in merging the two firms, it is found that some of the positions in one are duplicated in the other. Is it right to fire or demote executives holding those duplicate positions, many of whom have served their respective firms for years? A manufacturer that has grown rapidly in an expanding market was helped greatly during that growth by wholesale distributors that introduced its products to retail stores. Now the market has become large enough to make direct distribution from the factory to the store in truckload lots much less expensive, and the market has become competitive enough to make the cost savings from direct distribution much more meaningful. Is it proper to change distribution channels? A paper company in northern Maine can generate power and reduce its energy costs by building a large dam on land that it owns, but the dam will block a river that canoeists and vacationers have used for years. Is it fair to ruin recreational opportunities for others?

"Right" and "proper" and "fair" are ethical terms. They express a judgment about our behavior towards other people that is felt to be just. We believe that there are right and wrong ways to behave toward others, proper and improper actions, fair and unfair decisions. These beliefs are our moral standards of behavior. They reflect our sense of obligation to other people, our sense that it is better to help rather than to harm other people. The problem, however, is that frequently it is difficult to avoid harming other people, and this is particularly true in business management. Why? Various groups are involved in business—managers at different levels and functions, workers of different skills and backgrounds, suppliers of different materials, distributors of different products, creditors of different types, stockholders of different holdings, and citizens of different communities, states, and countries—and benefits for one group frequently result in harms for others.

We can illustrate this problem of mixed benefits and harms with examples from the introductory paragraph. It would seem wrong at first glance to fire executives who happened, through no fault of their own, to hold duplicate positions in the merged firms; yet let us assume that the two companies were in a very competitive industry and that the basic reason for the merger was to become more efficient and to be better able to withstand foreign competitors. What will happen if the staff reductions are not made? Who will be hurt, then, among other managers, workers, suppliers, distributors, creditors, stockholders, and members of the local communities? Who will benefit if the company is unable to survive? Even if survival is not an issue, who will benefit if the company is unable to grow or if it lacks the resources necessary for product research and market development? The basic questions are the same in the other two examples: Who will benefit, and how much? Who will be penalized, and how much? These are easy questions to ask, but difficult ones to resolve. In many instances, fortunately, alternatives can be considered. Duplicate managers, instead of being fired, might be retrained and reassigned. Inefficient distributors are a more difficult problem, though a place might be made for them by introducing new products or developing new markets or allowing them to participate in the new distribution processes. The dam across the waterway poses the most difficult problem: it either exists or it doesn't, and making it smaller or putting it in a different location does not really resolve the dilemma.

MORAL PROBLEMS AS MANAGERIAL DILEMMAS

Moral problems are truly managerial dilemmas. They represent a conflict between an organization's economic performance (measured by revenues, costs, and profits) and its social performance (stated in terms of obligations to persons both within and outside the organization). The nature of these obligations is, of course, open to interpretation, but most of us would agree that they include protecting loyal employees, maintaining competitive markets, and producing safe products and services.

Unfortunately, the dilemma of management is that these obligations are costly, both for organizations evaluated by financial standards and for managers subject to financial controls. The manufacturer that distributes direct from the factory to stores will be more profitable and better able to withstand competition than the manufacturer that ships to wholesale warehouses for additional handling and transport. The salesperson, to use a new and more troublesome illustration, who gives small bribes to purchasing agents will have a better record and receive higher commissions than the salesperson who refuses to countenance unethical payments. The design engineer who finds ways to sharply reduce material costs is more likely to be promoted than the design engineer who places product quality and consumer safety above cost considerations. There is a "right" or "proper" or "just" balance between economic performance and social performance, and the dilemma of management comes in finding it. The purpose of this book is to examine the factors that enter into that balance and to consider various theoretical structures—economic theories, legal regulations, and philosophic doctrines—that may assist management in determining it.

It is possible, of course, to ignore the balance between economic and social performance and to argue that the managerial dilemma does not exist. This argument has been advanced from two opposite directions. Some contend that management should concentrate entirely on economic performance. This view is almost a caricature of the 19th-century approach to business, in which coal mines were assumed to be unsafe and steel mills were expected to produce pollution as well as profits. Fortunately, this belief seems to be not at all common today; most managers recognize the impact of their decisions and actions upon other members of the organization and other citizens within the community. Some people may wish that the managers made other decisions or took other actions, but I think that it is necessary to admit that the recognition of moral responsibility does exist. There are few executives active now in either business firms or nonprofit institutions who do not understand the far reaching consequences of their decisions and, to some extent, act upon that understanding.

The second view, which is far more widespread, comes from an oversimplification of the issue of social performance. Those who hold this view might say, for example, with some degree of asperity, that "no company should discharge harmful wastes, pay illegal bribes, or produce unsafe products" and might then declare, with an equal degree of satisfaction, that "those ethical difficulties have been resolved—let us go on to the more interesting and nationally critical problems of the proper utilization of our scarce resources." This view ignores the subtlety of ethical issues in management; it assumes that ethical questions have only a "yes" side and a "no" side and that explicit economic benefits and definite social costs are associated with each of these two alternatives, so that only a very simple level of moral understanding is needed to make the proper choice. In fact, however, ethical questions can have many alternatives, each with different economic and social consequences, some with unknown probabilities of occurrence, and most with personal impacts upon the managers. Let us look at some of these more complex ethical problems.

A MORAL DILEMMA IN ENVIRONMENTAL PROTECTION

The exhaust from a diesel engine contains approximately 900 chemical compounds. Most of these compounds have been identified, but the environmental effects of only a few of the compounds have been studied. It seems safe to assume that some of the chemical compounds in diesel exhaust are harmful to human health or to air quality. It also seems safe to assume that in total the exhaust from a diesel engine is less harmful than that from a gasoline motor due to the absence of lead compounds—there is some lead even in "lead-free gasoline"—and to the lower levels of nitrous oxides. Every diesel engine manufacturer has a laboratory group that is studying the impact of the exhaust gases upon the general ecological system. Let us assume that in one of these companies this laboratory group finds that a particular compound is very deleterious to roadside vegetation. What are the managers of that company to do?

The managers of this diesel engine manufacturer have a number of choices, all with very uncertain outcomes, that interrelate economic, social, environmental, and personal factors. If they stop producing diesel engines, they will harm their own employees, suppliers, dealers, customers, and owners, and they will probably cause even greater deterioration in air quality as gasoline engines replace the discontinued diesel units. If they develop, at considerable cost, a catalytic converter to reduce or eliminate the harmful compound and then raise their prices, they may be less able to compete within the market. If they absorb the costs of the catalytic converter as a contribution to national welfare, the reduced profits would probably cause increased resistance in labor wage negotiations. In any case, is it ethical to shift the burden from society in general to factory workers in particular? "Aha," you retort, "that will not be necessary; the managers can certainly advise the responsible people within the federal government and allow a regulatory agency to establish industry-wide standards, so that all producers will compete with the same cost and price structure." Fine, but now what is to be done about the international market? Forty percent of the diesel engines manufactured in the United States are sold abroad or are installed in domestic equipment that is then sold abroad. If these standards are extended internationally for U.S. producers, they will probably be unable to compete abroad, with all the consequences of that inability upon economies of scale and costs of production for the domestic market. If these standards are not extended internationally for U.S. producers, an implicit statement is made that foreign people are of less worth than people in the United States.

Ethical issues are complex. Let us look at one or two others. Fortunately, these problems are interesting as well as intricate.

A MORAL DILEMMA IN FOREIGN BRIBERY

Bribery is generally considered reprehensible. Even in countries where it is alleged to be common, most people deplore it, except at the lower levels of some governmental bureaucracies where bribes are regarded as part of the compensation system, almost on a level with commissions or gratuities. Probably the principal reason for the widespread condemnation of bribery is its inherent inequity; it is obviously unfair to have special payments and secret influence decide issues that should be decided on their merits. All ethical systems recognize the need for equity; all ethical systems deplore the practice of bribery. It is interesting to note that one of the earliest written ethical beliefs, "Crito" in *The Dialogues of Socrates*, discussed bribery and recognized the dilemma that an act which is prima facie—that is, at first glance, before considering the full ramifications—considered to be wrong, such as bribery, can result in ends which are prima facie considered to be good, such as the release of an unjustly convicted prisoner. This same dilemma, though perhaps on a less dramatic scale, exists in management.

Let us look first at a small and almost routine transaction. Assume that the manager of a Brazilian subsidiary of an American company has received a notice that a shipment of repair parts has been delivered to the Sao Paulo docks and is being held by the customs officials. The common practice is to hire a Brazilian agent who specializes in clearing imports through customs; such agents are considered semi-professionals, with some legal and financial training, but they are known primarily for their good verbal abilities and their superb negotiating skills. They tend to be quick-witted people who understand the interests of their opponents, and they strive for a fast determination of the applicable import fees and an early release of the impounded goods. After a shipment has been cleared through customs, the agent submits a bill that includes an amount for the duty and a charge for the negotiations. This charge varies, but not with the size of the duty: a commission at a set percentage of the duty would be considered "unethical" in Brazil. In that country it is thought that the agent is responsible for negotiating the lowest possible duty for his or her client, which of course would result in the lowest possible income for him- or herself if the fee were based upon a percentage of the duty. Consequently it is felt to be "wrong" to force agents to choose between their own interests and the interests of their clients. Instead, the charge depends on the time needed to complete the transaction: the quicker the work, the higher the payment. It is assumed that part of the agent's fee has been paid to the customs officials; the larger payments, of course, bring more prompt attention from the officials and much quicker release of the goods. Payments on this basis also serve the interests of the client, for delays in Brazilian customs can extend from two to three months.

In this example, the ethical issue is slightly blurred, partially because there is no proof that bribery payments have been made—though it is logical to assume that some exchange has occurred to gain the attention of the customs officials—and partially because this exchange has been indirect. Managers in the subsidiary of the American company can legally claim that they have not paid bribes, though I am not certain that this claim would be considered defensible by those of us outside the courtroom. The ethical problem, though blurred, seems clear enough: Should a company employ an agent who will probably bribe a government official, resulting in inequitable treatment for others and favored treatment for itself?

Most ethical issues in management are at this apparently simple level: there is a dichotomous, yes or no choice, with relatively clear financial benefits and social obligations associated with each alternative, and the solution proposed is to sensitize people trained in financial analysis to recognize and include social costs in that analysis. But, as stated earlier, this seems to oversimplify the ethical dilemma and to ignore many of the complexities of managerial ethics.

Let us add some of those complexities to the present illustration. Let us assume that the repair parts in question are needed to maintain a communication system, or a manufacturing plant, or even a health-care facility. If the parts are not cleared promptly through customs and a breakdown occurs, people may be inconvenienced because of a failure of the communication system, or they may be unemployed because of a shutdown of the manufacturing plant, or they may suffer death or severe pain because of a breakdown in service at a hospital. Now it becomes clear that the comparison of financial benefits versus social costs is neither as simple nor as obvious as it appeared earlier, for the social ramifications of the decision extend beyond the first level of results into subsequent levels. The consequences of managerial decisions, even on such day-to-day issues as the customs clearance of imported goods, extend throughout society, and these consequences, both positive and negative, have to be included in the original analysis.

Let us also agree that the problem being discussed, paying an indirect bribe for prompt customs clearance, is not truly dichotomous. Numerous alternatives in addition to the obvious yes and no choices are also available. The subsidiary could engage in forward planning and order repair parts far in advance of actual need so that the lengthy delays in customs could be tolerated and the need to pay bribes eliminated. Statistical analysis of the operations, whether of a communication system, a manufacturing plant, or a health-care facility, would indicate a probable demand for repair parts, and numerous mathematical models are available to establish adequate inventory levels, given lengthy delivery times. Another alternative would be to have a corporate attorney negotiate with the customs officials, subject to explicit policy instructions not to pay bribes under any circumstances, and force the officials through legal penalties to clear shipments in the order of their arrival. Yet another alternative would be to obtain repair parts from local suppliers, thus helping to bolster the national economy while avoiding the problems of customs clearance entirely.

Each of these alternatives has a financial cost that we can assume will be somewhat greater than the expenses for the currently minimal bribes, but that cost can be computed. So, on the surface, it would appear that we are now looking at a comparison of financial costs versus social benefits. But, to the manager who has to decide, it is very obvious that here each alternative has a social cost that is more subtle. The inventory models require, for computation, an estimate of the costs of lacking a part that is needed for repairs. The original intent of the management scientists who developed these models was to consider only objective judgments of the costs to the company, but it has become obvious in recent years that the models also have to include subjective estimates of the costs to the employees, the customers, and the general population. Even unsophisticated management science procedures now require some estimate of the costs external to the firm and of the economic damages caused by the firm. In the particular instance being discussed, what cost should be included for Brazilian people who are being inconvenienced when their communication system breaks down due to lack of repair parts? What cost should be included for Brazilian workers who become unemployed and unpaid when their factory is shut down? What cost should be included for Brazilian patients who are untreated when their hospital is unable to function? These are not simple financial estimates; they are extended social costs that are difficult to compute but have to be included in ethical managerial decisions, even when management science procedures are being used. Ethical managerial issues are also posed by the other two alternatives that were suggested—employing a corporate attorney to force the customs official to adhere to the provisions of the law even if this resulted in court actions and civil penalties against those officials, and purchasing repair parts within the country, even if this required an uneconomic transfer of both capital and technology to a local company. If the former alternative were chosen, a corporate attorney would be hired to impose American standards of bureaucratic integrity upon the Brazilian civil service. At one level, there is the question whether an American firm has the right to force its views upon others. At a more subtle level, we have to look at the social structure of Brazil. Corporate attorneys there tend to come from the wealthier families, while customs officials are members of a much poorer class. In essence, the company would be transferring payments from the poor to the rich and thereby helping to maintain the inequitable social divisions of South America.

The sourcing of repair parts within the country seems an attractive alternative superficially, but it involves moving jobs from the United States to Brazil, along with the proprietary technology and some capital investment. That movement will doubtless be directly counter to employee expectations—if not union contracts—in the United States. Until recently, union negotiators seldom foresaw the possibility of foreign purchases of complex components, believing the necessary technical

skills to be absent in low-wage-rate areas. With the continual development of advanced technologies in less developed countries that situation has changed. Using foreign labor may create worker hardships in
the United States.

Having examined the extended impacts, multiple alternatives, and
mixed outcomes that seem to be inherently associated with ethical decisions in management, we will now consider two additional levels of
complexity, and then it will be possible to present a series of conclusions on the nature of ethics in management. The fourth level of complexity is the uncertain consequences of managerial decisions. When a
managerial decision is made, it is seldom clear exactly what the
outcome of that decision will be, and unfortunately the greatest clarity
often seems to be linked to the least ethical action, judged by prima
facie standards. In the simple illustration that has been used throughout
this section—the payment of an indirect bribe to facilitate the clearance
of repair parts through customs—it is reasonable to assume that if the
bribe is paid, the shipment will be released. The Brazilian customs officials may be unfamiliar with the cynical 19th-century American aphorism,
"An honest man is one who, once bribed, stays bought." However, they
doubtless understand that unless agreements concluded with the import
agents are observed (one hesitates to say "honored" in this context), further
negotiations and payments will be impaired. An equal certainty does not
extend to the other alternatives.

Uncertainty is even present in the alternative of an expanded repair
parts inventory. We have all been annoyed by delays in repair service caused by inadequate inventories; such inadequacies can stem from
management inattention, financial constraints, or pure chance. Most of
them can probably be ascribed to the first two causes, but a combination
of rare events is always a possibility, particularly in repair service where
numerous parts are needed for each operating system, where a given region
or area contains multiple operating systems, and where obtaining repair
parts is subject to extensive delays. Murphy's Law has not been
repealed by management science, it has just been partially circum-
vented; and even large, economically unjustifiable inventories cannot
prevent downtime caused by a lack of parts. This is the dilemma that the
manager of every repair service intuitively understands: he or she is unable
to assure complete protection against failure. That inability is annoying
when the parts are needed by a communication system, troublesome when
they are needed by a manufacturing plant, and depressing when they are
needed by a hospital.

Formal procedures for including uncertainty are available for inventory-
planning models, based upon the statistical analysis of historical operating patterns, but such procedures are not applicable to the other two
alternatives that were suggested, since relevant data points are lacking.
It is not at all clear what would happen if an attorney threatened or insti-

tuted legal action against customs officials in Brazil. Those officials might release the shipments promptly to avoid harassment in a legal system they did not understand—or papers might be lost, hearings delayed, and shipments misdirected as the same officials created havoc in an import system they understood very well indeed.

An incident illustrates how the legal system can be confounded. I have been told that a Brazilian attorney watched customs officials unwrap, inspect, and clear for import 20 fuel injectors for large diesel engines. The fuel injector is a precisely machined component in the engine; it tends to wear out because of the high pressures that are required in operation. The fuel injectors were inspected, cleared, shipped, and stored. After the first one was installed on an engine, it was found that a pinch of very fine sand had been deposited in the input ports of each unit. All of them had to be scrapped. Sabotage is not common, in Brazil or elsewhere, but it does happen; a manager has to recognize that it can occur and plan for that possibility.

It is also not at all clear what would happen if a local company were selected and trained to produce the needed repair parts inside the country. The training would probably extend far beyond simple instruction in manual skills, requiring the importation of advanced equipment for both production and testing and the explanation of managerial processes in operations scheduling, test evaluation, and quality control. Despite technological and financial assistance from the parent firm, and assuming goodwill and effort on the part of all others, the exportation of highly technical processes is often unsuccessful; it requires a degree of precision and skill that may be outside the culture of the receiving firm.

In summary, it is not certain that the necessary repair parts can be manufactured in Brazil, despite the investment of money and effort. It is also not certain that they can be imported into Brazil by pressuring the customs officials with legal penalties. It is, however, reasonably certain that these parts can be received promptly by employing an import agent and authorizing the customary payments. Uncertainty seems to be a constant companion of the ethical approach to management.

The last level of complexity that we will consider is the personal involvement of the managers. It seems reasonable to assume that this involvement is partially an emotional concern with the ethical dilemma—no one likes to pay bribes or to conspire in their indirect payment—but that it is primarily a practical worry over the impact of ethical issues upon the manager's salary, promotion, and career. Managers, particularly those in autonomous operating units some distance from the corporate headquarters, are expected to "get things done" and to "keep things running." They are not told that they are free to do whatever is necessary to accomplish those goals, and many corporations have definite ethical codes and specific functional policies that attempt to preclude many actions, but the managerial controls tend to emphasize financial results and not ethical decisions. The ability of managers to "keep things running" will show up on the control system during the next quarter, while the decisions and actions that enabled them to do so have to be explained verbally, if at all. Managerial controls tend to focus on the short term and the obvious but they are often used in judgments about longer-term salaries and promotions.

Managers in almost all companies operate within the constraints of a control system. Certainly, managers in all well-run companies operate within such constraints, and it does no harm to assume that the American manufacturing firm with a troubled subsidiary in Brazil is well run. The controls are normally based upon a comparison of actual results with planned objectives. These objectives are usually set by an extrapolation of past results, with some adjustment for current conditions and local problems derived through discussions between the responsible managers. Both results and objectives are focused primarily on financial measures such as sales revenues, variable costs, fixed expenses, and the resultant profits or losses, because those are the figures that are available from the accounting records. Assuming that the Brazilian subsidiary has this kind of control system, that failure to provide adequate repair service will eventually affect sales revenues, and assuming that payments to the import agent can be classified as a legitimate and necessary business expense, it must be a rare manager who would not say, "Damn the company for putting me into this position," and make the call authorizing indirect payments. This is unfortunate, but it happens, and I think that it is necessary to understand the behavioral implications of the control system that help to make it happen.

CHARACTERISTICS OF MORAL PROBLEMS IN MANAGEMENT

What does all this mean? We have examined in great detail a relatively minor problem faced by a worried manager primarily to consider in detail the actual nature of the moral dilemma in management. From that examination, five conclusions concerning the complexity of managerial ethics can be stated simply and directly:

1. Most ethical decisions have extended consequences. The results of managerial decisions and actions do not stop with the first-level consequences. Rather, these results extend throughout society, and that extension constitutes the essence of the ethical argument: the decisions of managers have an impact upon others—both within the organization and within the society—that is beyond their control and that therefore should be considered when the decisions are made. Bribes change governmental processes. Pollution affects environmental health. Unsafe products destroy individual lives. There is little disagreement here; most people recognize the extended consequences of managerial actions. The disagreement results from the existence of the multiple alternatives, mixed outcomes, uncertain occurrences, and personal implications that complicate the decision process leading to those actions.

2. Most ethical decisions have multiple alternatives. It is commonly thought that ethical issues in management are primarily dichotomous, a yes and a no choice but no other alternatives. Should a manager pay a bribe or not? Should a factory pollute the air or not? Should a company manufacture unsafe products or not? Although a dichotomous framework presents the ethical issues in sharp contrast, it does not accurately reflect the managerial dilemma. As has been seen in the simple illustration of bribery payments for import clearances, and as will be shown in numerous other examples throughout this text, multiple alternatives have to be considered in making ethical choices.

3. Most ethical decisions have mixed outcomes. It is commonly thought that ethical issues in management are largely antithetical, with directly opposed financial returns and social costs. Pay an indirect bribe, but maintain the sales volume of imported goods through prompt delivery. Cause some air or water pollution, but avoid the costs of installing and operating pollution control equipment. Design a slightly unsafe product, but reduce the material and labor costs of manufacture. Like the dichotomous framework, the antithetical model for outcome evaluation presents the ethical issues in sharp focus but does not accurately portray the managerial dilemma. Social benefits and costs as well as financial revenues and expenses are associated with almost all of the alternatives in ethical choices.

4. Most ethical decisions have uncertain consequences. It is commonly thought that ethical issues in management are free of risk or doubt, with a known outcome for each alternative. Pay the bribe, and receive the imported goods promptly. Invest in pollution control equipment, and the emissions will be reduced X percent at Y costs of operation. Produce an absolutely safe product at an additional cost of Z dollars per unit. A deterministic model—that is, one without probabilities—simplifies the process of analysis, but it does not accurately describe the managerial dilemma. It was not at all clear what consequences would follow from the alternatives considered to avoid paying indirect bribes to Brazilian customs officials; it is not at all clear what consequences will follow from most ethical choices.

5. Most ethical decisions have personal implications. It is commonly thought that ethical issues in management are largely impersonal, divorced from the lives and careers of the managers. Many people believe that prima facie ethical decisions in a given operation may reduce the profits of the company but not the executives' salaries or their opportunities for promotion. Managerial controls, however, are designed to record financial results of the operations, not the ethical quality of the decisions that led to those results, and most incentive systems are based upon these controls. Maintain the dollar sales of imported goods at expected levels, and despite slightly increased expenses for indirect bribes, the quarterly review will be pleasant and remunerative. Delay the installation of pollution control equipment, and the return on invested capital will be close to the planned percentage. Redesign the product to reduce material and labor costs, and profit margins and the chances of promotion will increase. An impersonal model certainly simplifies the process of decision on ethical issues, but it far from accurately describes the managerial dilemma. Individual benefits and costs, as well as financial and social benefits and costs, are associated with most of the alternatives in ethical decisions.

EXAMPLES OF MORAL PROBLEMS IN MANAGEMENT

Moral problems in management are complex because of the extended consequences, multiple alternatives, mixed outcomes, uncertain occurrences, and personal implications. Moral problems in management are also pervasive, because managers make decisions and take actions that will affect other people. If those decisions and actions affect other people adversely, if they hurt or harm those people in ways beyond their individual control, then we have an moral problem that requires some degree of ethical analysis in addition to the more common economic analysis. What are some of these moral problems? Let us look at a few, bearing in mind that the balance of benefits versus harms differs for each, and that each of us will probably differ in our view of the moral correctness of that balance. That is, using once again the ethical issues discussed in the introductory paragraph of this chapter, some of us may feel that it is morally wrong to discharge long-service employees following a merger, to replace wholesale distributors as the market matures, or to build a power-generating dam that will block recreational access to a river. Others of us may feel that some decisions of this kind are morally wrong but that some decisions—particularly the dam on company-owned private property—are morally right. Still others among us may argue that while all of these decisions do have harmful consequences to some people, they are nonetheless all morally right.

Our evaluations of the moral correctness of each action will differ because our moral standards of behavior upon which those evaluations are based also differ. Our moral standards are our intuitive judgments about the "rightness" or "wrongness" of actions. They are based upon our value judgments of purpose, or what we feel to be truly important in life. Both our moral standards and our value judgments in turn are dependent upon our religious and cultural traditions and our economic and social situations. Young people in a desperately poor country such as Bangladesh where jobs are very scarce are going to feel differently about whether or not it is "right" to cause some air and water pollution in a factory that employs hundreds of workers than are young people in a comparatively wealthy country such as the United States. Those in the United States, in turn are going to feel differently about that same issue than are young people in some of the native cultures that have traditionally shown great respect for the land and limited respect for wealth.

These relationships between an individual's moral standards and value judgments and the cultural/religious traditions and the economic/social situations of that same individual can be shown very simply in graphic format in Exhibit 1–1.

Ethical principles of analysis are very different from either moral standards of behavior or value judgments of purpose or priority. Ethical principles are not subjective. They do not vary with religious and cultural traditions or with economic and social situations. Instead, they are ways of thinking about what is best for society. This book will discuss, in the next three chapters, three alternative ways of thinking about what is best for society: economic theories, legal regulations, and philosophical doctrines.

Those three approaches to determining what is best for society are not important at this stage of the discussion. What is important at this stage is to recognize that each of the decisions and actions that will be described briefly below can affect other people adversely, can hurt or harm them in ways beyond their control, and consequently have a moral content. Hurt or harm to others in ways outside their own control is the essential element in the moral dilemma of management. That condition is present in all the examples that follow.

Before going on to describe these additional moral problems in management, let me state two qualifications and provide one explanation. First, the intent is not to describe every possible instance in which managerial decisions and actions can hurt or harm individuals in ways beyond their control. Rather, the intent is to provide a limited number of examples that show the pervasive nature of ethical issues in management and furnish general topics for subsequent discussions of the various analytical means for reaching decisions when confronted with these moral problems.

Second, the intent is not to describe dramatic and well-publicized instances of management decisions that were clearly unethical and often illegal as well. The president of Lockheed did pay $3.2 million to

Exhibit 1–1

The Relationship between Morals, Values, and Ethics

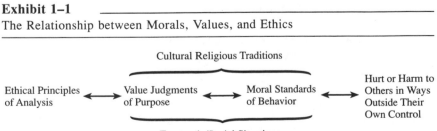

various government officials and representatives of the prime minister of Japan to ensure the purchase of 20 passenger planes by the Japanese national airline.[1] Senior members of management at General Dynamics did add $63 million of improper overhead expenses, including country club memberships and dog kennel fees, to defense contracts over a two year period.[2] Regional managers at E. F. Hutton did issue bank overdrafts that gave Hutton the interest-free use of up to $250 million and cost banks as much as $8 million.[3] In a case that seems unbelievably outrageous, marketing and production executives at the Beech-Nut Baby Foods Company did conspire to substitute a chemical concoction with artificial sweetners for natural apple juice in one of the company's major product lines.[4] These unethical actions did occur, but few people would defend them except perhaps to say that one has to adopt foreign business practices when doing business abroad, or that the Defense Department is too large to properly control costs, or that the banks should have recognized what was happening much earlier and taken appropriate action. No one, I think it is safe to assume, would attempt to provide a similar excuse for tampering with food products destined for very young children. The intent, however, is not to look at such famous moral lapses on the part of very senior executives. Rather, the intent is to look at a range of ethical issues at the operating, middle, and strategic levels of management and in a variety of the functional and technical specialties. Some of these issues require decisions by senior executives, but most are the routine, even mundane decisions and actions that lower-level managers—and recent graduates of business schools—face on an almost daily basis.

Last, and this is the explanation that I feel that I should make, I am going to use anonymous quotations to amplify and support some of the descriptions of these moral problems in management. This is in direct contradiction to the research rule that sources should always be cited, so that the validity of the findings can be substantiated. However, I believe that in this instance the use of anonymous quotations may be justified. It is difficult to get examples of ethical problems at the lower and middle levels of management. Managers at those levels do not like to discuss the moral dilemmas they have faced, for the obvious reason that those discussions can adversely affect their careers. They will discuss them only with persons who are known to have an interest in the area, who perhaps can help them in the resolution of the problem, and who certainly will maintain confidentiality. I have taught at four schools of business administration over the past 20 years, and at each of these institutions I have either conducted short seminars or used short cases in elective classes that revealed my interest in the ethics of management. Former students from those seminars and classes occasionally contact me when troubled about particular practices that seem to be accepted as ordinary business routines within their companies. They write or speak with the assumption of confidentiality, and so I cannot identify them. Yet their descriptions are much more vivid, and probably valid, than my own because they have been part of the problems they are describing, and so I wish to include the descriptions. That is the reason I believe the use of anonymous quotations is justified in these examples. Now, on to the problems.

Pricing Level

Price, it would seem, should be a purely economic decision based upon cost and demand. Yet the pricing level selected can have harmful effects upon some customers. In banking, for example, under the combined impact of deregulation by the government and competition from other financial service firms, it has become common to pay fairly high rates of interest on customer deposits above a given size. The benefits of those rates go primarily to the customers with the larger bank balances. To offset the increased interest that must be paid to attract the larger deposits and to reflect the actual costs of service, most banks have raised the fees they charge smaller customers.

> I have been asked to do a study of the pricing for our checking account services. Other banks in the area now charge $0.10 for each transaction for accounts that don't maintain a $1,000.00 balance and an additional $5.00 per month for the very small accounts with a balance that falls under $300.00. That makes a lot of sense, economically. We just barely break even now servicing the medium-sized accounts, and we lose money on the smaller ones. The proposed price changes would mean that our returns would be equal for all three sizes of accounts.

> But there is a problem. We are an urban bank. Many of our customers are retired, on Social Security. $5.00 a month plus $0.10 a transaction is a major expense for them; it may well represent a couple of meals that they are not going to eat. Most of them don't have the money to maintain a $300 balance, let alone the $1,000 amount. They're older, and frightened of carrying cash. I don't think that it is right to, in essence, deny checking account services to older people, but I don't know what to do about it. You see, if we don't have the same rate structure as the other banks, we will get all of these older and unprofitable customers.

> When I left [name of the business school], I was determined that I would maintain my personal standards in everything that I did. Yet in the first year I am going to recommend a policy that I think is morally wrong. (Statement of former student)

Distribution Channels

Retail distribution has changed dramatically over the last ten years with the growth of big discount chains such as K-Mart and Wal-Mart and the start of national specialty stores such as Toys-R-Us and Home Depot. The latter are known as "category killers"; they tend to kill off small local shops selling the same category of merchandise due to their much larger selections and much lower prices. Both the big discount chains and the national specialty stores have a further advantage over their smaller competitors; they receive much better delivery service from the manufacturers. A recent graduate of a business school felt that this was "wrong":

> Theoretically a small toy store or fashion shop could survive if the owner knew his or her customers really well, and could anticipate what they would want before they wanted it. Each year some toys become very popular and some fashions for men as well as for women become very much in demand. The problem is that even if the owners did anticipate these changes in demand, and did order well in advance, if the items become popular enough their orders won't be shipped to them. Manufacturers will take care of their large customers first.

> Most people are willing to wait in line for service. The idea of "first come, first served" expresses a pretty widely accepted concept of very simple social justice. I would get upset if I was waiting in a line to buy a ticket or to board a bus and somebody else pushed in front of me, and yet this happens all the time in our dealings with the big chains. They just expect to come in front of everybody else. I don't like it but there is obviously nothing much I can do about it. (Statement of former student)

Advertising Messages

Truth in advertising is a complex issue, and an emotional one. A rigidly truthful television or magazine ad, every statement of which is supported by a reference to a scientific study, would be incredibly dull and probably ineffective. A totally untruthful television or magazine ad, with wildly exaggerated claims, would be illegal and probably equally ineffective. Varying degrees of truthfulness and deception lie between those two extremes. The problem for one former student was where to draw the line along that spectrum.

> Despite our reputation as hucksters, 90 percent of what we do in advertising is legitimate, and based upon valid market analysis. For the large majority of our clients, we act more as marketing consultants than as advertisers. Our ads may be dull; they are generally unimaginative; and they often present a very one-sided view of things, but they are seldom designed to be deliberately untruthful.

> It's the other 10 percent that I worry about. We have a client who says that they want a campaign with more "bite"; bite to them means more pull, more attraction to the buyer, even if that attraction is blatantly untrue and totally misrepresented. They are in the financial services industry, but they want to sell their products as if they were headache remedies or arthritis rubs. "Up 87 percent over the past three years" is the heading they have on a mutual fund ad, and that is an accurate statement only

if you stay strictly within that time frame; over the past five years the fund has not kept pace with the growth in the Dow Jones Averages. "8-1/2 percent interest" is the heading they have on a money market fund; there is a small asterisk, and down at the bottom of the page a footnote that explains the 8-1/2 percent is for the first three months only. "Insured by [name of an insurance company]" is a phrase they want on every ad that mentions customer accounts; that insurance company is their wholly owned and poorly funded subsidiary. We do the work for them, but I don't like it. (Statement of former student)

Working Conditions

The working conditions for many manual and clerical employees are less than ideal. Temperature, humidity, or noise levels may be too high; ventilation and lighting may be too low, and fumes and dust are still found in some workplaces. The most harmful of these conditions along with the obvious safety hazards, have been outlawed by state and federal laws, but there are still many opportunities to improve working conditions for hourly employees. Here is a former student who felt that it would harm his career to make such improvements.

   I think that all MBAs, and I'll include the BBAs too, should be forced as part of their education to work in a steel stamping plant or a gray iron foundry. The noise, the heat, the fumes, and the pace of work are close to intolerable. If there aren't enough places for all of them in a stamping plant or an iron foundry, you could put the balance of them "out on the line" [on the assembly line in an automobile factory].

   We have executives in this company who just don't understand what it is like to work under these conditions. Their offices are in New York, and they only come out here a couple of times a year to tell us that we're falling behind on the profit plan. I could put in a capital request to improve some of the worst conditions, but I would have to fight to get it approved. I'm not certain I want to make that effort; people who fight for capital projects that don't show a substantial internal rate of return tend not to get promoted around here. (Statement of former student)

Expense Controls

The annual payments of senior executives within the United States have escalated sharply in recent years. Many of the presidents and vice presidents of major companies listed on the New York Stock Exchange receive salaries that are well over $1,000,000 per year, plus bonuses for increases in sales or profits during their period of service, plus options to purchase stock at prices well below the current market. The total can easily amount to $2,000,000 to $3,000,000 annually, and amounts as high as $100,000,000 have been recorded. These payments to senior executives in the United States tend to be eight to ten times as high as to their counterparts in Europe or Japan. The chief executive of a major company in Japan might be paid $350,000 per year, for example; the person holding a similar position in Germany might receive $250,000.

The salaries, bonuses, and options of senior executives are disclosed publicly in the so-called "10-K" reports which by law must accompany each company's annual report. The expense accounts, however, are not disclosed, and some of these have been felt to be excessive.

> I work in the marketing department at [name of a large consumer products firm) and that, of course, is where the expense accounts of the senior executives are assigned. Who can begrudge money spent for marketing? But, much of this has no relationship to marketing. The expenses we get from headquarters are for family vacation tours, country club fees, sporting event tickets. In the 1992 Olympics held at Barcelona, Spain we paid for a chartered yacht that stayed right in the port and provided accommodations for visiting executives and their friends and family. We don't sell in Spain, and have limited business in Western Europe. There was no legitimate reason for our executives to be there, yet that four week charter cost us $125,000. I'm just an assistant sales manager, but I have to approve all of the expense accounts, including these from the senior executives. These are the same senior executives who, when asked publicly about the future of the company, say that what is needed is more hard work and personal sacrifice on the part of us all to meet the price competition of foreign firms from low wage-rate areas. Do the directors know what is going on? (Statement of former student)

Workforce Reductions

It has become common to reduce the size and the overhead cost of many large companies by discharging some of the employees, to create a "lean and mean" style of management. These "downsizing operations" or—as they are more euphemistically termed "rightsizing operations"—are often a response to an increase in competitive pressures, but there are obvious human costs to the people forced to leave.

> Our company, in August, is going to announce the firing of 24,000 workers, including 15,000 administrative employees. [Name of the company] has always had a reputation for job security, almost lifetime employment, so this announcement is going to come as a shock to many people.

> Of course, the older ones will get the option of early retirement. But the younger ones, in their 30s and 40s, are just going to get a few months' severance pay and some outplacement counseling. I am part of a task force that was set up to decide exactly what benefits should be given to the various longevity classes.

> The senior executives in this company had it easy. When they were at this level, the only problem they had was expansion: finding more people, training them, promoting them. They never had to deal with contraction;

they don't recognize the really agonizing nature of the decisions we have to make on an almost daily basis now. (Statement of former student)

Pollution Causes

Improper disposal of toxic wastes is clearly illegal, yet some companies continue to dump chemicals into public sewers or vacant lots despite possible harm to the environment and probable conflict with the law.

> I have been working for [name of the company] for about six months, at their [name of the city] plant. It is common practice here to pour used solvents and cleaning solutions down the storm drain. I asked the plant manager about it, and he said that this is legal in small amounts. I don't think that it is legal, and I don't think that the amounts are that small, but I'm not certain that I want to get involved at this stage of my career. (Statement of former student)

Community Relations

The major employer within a local community has substantial economic power, particularly if the employer has plants in other locations and can move work, and employment, among plants. This economic power often is used in pressing for tax reductions, which can have an obvious impact upon residents of the community by increasing their taxes or decreasing their services.

> [Name of the company] is pushing for a 50 percent tax reduction in [name of the city], where I live. Two years ago it got a 24 percent reduction. Now it is threatening to close the plant unless it gets the full amount. If that reduction goes through, it is going to increase taxes on my house by over $500 a year. I can afford it; I'm well paid. But there are older people around here, and some farmers, who are going to be driven right to the wall. Doesn't the company understand what it is doing? (Statement of former student)

Supplier Relations

Large manufacturing firms have economic power within the communities in which they operate, and against the small suppliers from which they purchase materials, parts, and supplies. Economic power is a difficult concept to define, but it is an easy force to recognize.

> This company has started to play hardball with our suppliers. People in purchasing think nothing of calling up a supplier we've worked with for years, and telling the supplier it has lost the business unless we get a 7 percent price reduction. Generally we can't make the parts at the prices that purchasing demands, so it is an empty threat. But the supplier doesn't know that;

they'll come back with a 3 percent reduction, we'll compromise eventually at 4.2 percent, but we've started to drive somebody else out of business. (Statement of former student)

ANALYSIS OF ETHICAL PROBLEMS IN MANAGEMENT

How do we decide on these and other ethical issues? You may regard some of the examples cited as simple instances of practical management—small suppliers to any large manufacturing company have to be competitive in their price quotations and quality standards, or they will lose the business, and this is particularly true of suppliers to the automobile companies attempting to meet foreign competition. But, is it necessary to lie to those suppliers in order to get them to reduce their quotations? You may regard others as outrageous abuses of power and position. It is hard to justify a 76% real estate tax break for a corporation given that will result in a substantial increase in the real estate taxes levied against the homes of community residents, or a substantial decrease in the services provided for those residents, assuming that the original assessments were made equitably. Large, nonbusiness expense accounts on top of high annual payments are equally awkward to defend. Yet, what would you do if you were actually there? Ethical decisions are easy to make when a person is not directly involved. From a distance, it is easy to review other people's actions and say, "Yes, that is right," or "No, that is wrong."

Ethical decisions are much more difficult to make when a person is directly involved in the situation. Put yourself in the position of the purchasing agent in the automobile company who had to lie to a supplier. Could you do it? If you did not do it, could you continue to work for that company? Put yourself in the position of the person who discovered that the company he worked for was pouring solvents and cleaning fluids down the drain. What would you do?

Suppose you were the former student who was concerned that the directors of his or her company did not know of the apparently excessive expense accounts being submitted by some of the senior executives. Should you report it? Certainly if sales people in that same company abused their expense accounts in a similar way, they would be disciplined and might be discharged. This is an internal issue, between the executives and the owners, and not an external issue between the company and its suppliers, distributors, or customers, but the principle remains the same. Do you have an obligation to the directors who represent the owners, or only to the senior executives who at some point will probably have to approve your next promotion?

Suppose you were the former student who had to decide on the proper pricing level for the checking account services offered by your bank. Now, how do you analyze the situation? Is it strictly a matter of costs and margins, or does the bank have some obligation to continue to provide checking account services to older members of the community, and do you have some obligation to make certain that that occurs? Suppose you were asked to set up policy guidelines for the employees to be discharged in a corporate downsizing operation; what standards would you use? Suppose you recognized that your company was producing unsafe products, or making illegal payments; how would you decide what action to take? You need a method of analysis, beyond your intuitive moral standards, when confronted with an immediate ethical problem.

Ethical decisions are not simple choices between right and wrong; they are complex judgments on the balance between the economic performance and the social performance of an organization. In all the instances described above, except for the apparent managerial dishonesty in the example of the expense accounts, the economic performance of the organization, measured by revenues, costs, and profits, will be improved. In all the instances described above, the social performance of the organization—much more difficult to measure, but expressed as obligations to managers, workers, customers, suppliers, distributors, and members of the local community—will be reduced. People are going to be hurt. There has to be a balance between economic and social performance. How do you reach this balance? Three methods of analysis are relevant: economic, legal, and ethical.

Economic Analysis

It is possible to look at many of the problems that have been described as having a definite ethical content from the point of view of microeconomic theory, relying on impersonal market forces to make the decision between economic and social performance. Workforce reductions and plant closings are admittedly unpleasant for the workers who lose their jobs, but there is a labor market, and these workers will be employed again, provided they are willing to adjust their wage demands to market conditions. The small wholesalers that are going to be replaced by direct factory shipments to retail stores doubtless feel troubled, but their costs are too high; bring those costs down to a competitive level, and they will not be replaced. The underlying belief is that a society has a limited number of resources and that when consumers are supplied with highest quality goods at lowest possible costs, then those resources are being used as efficiently as possible and members of the society are being served as effectively as possible.

Legal Analysis

It is also possible to look at each of the problems that have an ethical content using the framework of legal theory, relying on impersonal social forces to make the choice between "right" and "wrong." Workforce reductions and plant closings are unpleasant, but society has never felt that they were so harmful to the people involved that a law prohibiting them was required.

Should they become a major problem, a law can be passed to deal with the situation. The small wholesalers that are going to be replaced doubtless feel badly, but they may have an implicit contract from their earlier service. They can sue in a court of law; if they win, they will not be replaced. The underlying belief here is that a democratic society can establish its own rules and that if people and organizations follow those rules, then members of that society will be treated as justly as possible.

Ethical Analysis

Lastly, it is possible to look at each of the problems that have a moral content using the structure of normative philosophy, relying on basic principles to make the choice between "right" and "wrong." Workforce reductions and plant closings, again, are unpleasant, but we can compute "the greatest good for the greatest number" and decide on that basis. The small wholesalers that are to be replaced are unhappy, but we can set up a rule that every organization, faced with an equivalent situation, has to act in the same way—Kant's Categorical Imperative—and thus achieve consistent and equitable behavior. The belief underlying normative philosophy is that if all the rational men and women in a society acted on the same principles of either beneficiency or consistency, then members of that society would be treated as fairly as possible.

Three methods of analysis have been proposed to resolve ethical dilemmas in management. The next three chapters will examine these methods in considerably greater detail.

Footnotes

1. "Japan: An Aftershock of the Lockheed Affair," *Business Week*, April 12, 1976, p. 43.

2. Roger Bennett, "Profile of Harry Crown, Founder of General Dynamics, Inc.," *New York Times*, June 16, 1985, p. 26f.

3. Scott McMurray, "Battered Broker: E.F. Hutton Appears Headed for Long Siege in Bank-Draft Scheme," *The Wall Street Journal*, July 12, 1985.

4. "What Led Beech-Nut Down the Road to Disgrace," *Business Week*, February 22, 1988, p. 124.

Case 1–1

Five Moral Problems Encountered by Members of One BBA Class

Students in a BBA class on the ethics of management at the University of Michigan were asked to submit a written description of a moral problem they had encountered at work over the previous summer. This was a voluntary assignment. Obviously, if they had not encountered a moral problem, or if they had encountered one that they felt they could not describe without violating the implied confidence of their prior employers, they did not have to participate. Nineteen problems were submitted. The following five were selected by members of the class for discussion at one of the subsequent meetings:

1. *Reporting inaccurate income.* "I didn't get the job I wanted, so I worked as a waitress at a restaurant in a vacation resort. We got room and board, the absolute minimum wage (with a charge deducted for the room and board), and tips. Tip income was very good because it was a popular restaurant, right on the shore, with really good food and above-average prices. The owner told us that it was our responsibility to report our tip income to the IRS when we filled out our income tax forms for the year, but he also said that he had to provide the government with an estimate at the end of the summer, based upon credit card charges, and then he gave us a figure for that estimate that was less than half of what I actually made. Now I have to file the return, and I need the money. What figure should I put down?"

2. *Misleading retail customers.* "I spent the summer working as a telephone sales representative at a travel agency. Customers would call, and say where they wanted to go. We would look up flights and times and fares on the computer, and help the customer pick the one that seemed best. That part was all right. But, often they asked us to reserve a rental car or find a hotel room. Here the problem was that there generally was a contest for the sales representative who could reserve the most cars from a particular rental firm or send the most clients to a specific hotel chain. All of those companies run contests like that, and the prizes they offer are not cheap. If I booked just 25 clients for (name of a car rental firm) during one month, my name would be put in a drawing for $2,500. If I booked 100 clients, the drawing was for $10,000. If I booked 200, I received a three-day Florida vacation free; there was no drawing. All of the other clerks participated in the contests, and the owner didn't seem to mind. The problem, of course,

was that the rates to the customers were higher than they would have been had we searched for the best deal for them rather than the best prize for us. The other clerks said I was crazy not to participate. Should I have participated?"

3. *Misleading industrial customers.* "I worked in the office of a company that distributed repair parts for heavy machinery throughout northern Michigan. When somebody would call in for a part, we would look up the number and price and inventory level on the computer. The boss told us always to say that we had the part in stock, even if the inventory level showed that we were out, that we didn't have any left. His argument was that we could always get the part from a large warehouse in Chicago in a day or two, and that if we did not say this the customer would just call that large warehouse in Chicago themselves. I didn't like it because it meant that I had to lie to somebody about once a day, but I don't suppose it really hurt anyone. What do you think I should have done?"

4. *Reporting employee theft.* "I worked in the shipping bay of a company that manufactured house paint. House paint in one gallon cans is a product you can sell easily in your neighborhood if you can just get it out the factory door; everyone needs paint. House paint in one gallon cans is also an easy product to get out the factory door; its a big volume product, and no one seems to keep exact track of the numbers of cans. When we were making up the pallets to load a truck—the cans of paint were put in cartons that held 4 cans, and then 20 cartons were strapped onto a wooden pallet that could be handled by a forklift—you could easily set aside a couple of cans. Then, when the foreman was on break and the office people were all working in the front of the building, you could just carry it out and put it in the trunk of your car. Most of the shipping crew did that once or twice a week. They felt the company owned it to them. I didn't because I didn't want to run the risk of being caught and having that put on my record. But, I didn't object when they gave me a couple of cans to use on my mother's home. And, I didn't tell the management of the company about it either. What should I have done?"

5. *Misusing employee time.* "This did not happen last summer. It happened a couple of summers ago. I was part of the maintenance crew for the Parks and Recreation Department in the town where I lived. We mowed the grass on the parks and athletic fields, and picked up the trash and did some painting and repair work. The problem was that we not only did the parks and athletic fields, we also did the lawns and gardens of some of the people in the city government, the school system, and the athletic department. I mowed the lawn of the football coach every week until practice started. He used to tell me I'd never make the team unless I could move faster on the football field than I did on his front lawn, but he always gave me a glass of lemonade and a $5.00 tip when I was finished.

I never thought about it until I took this course, but maybe it wasn't right to use city employees to work on private property."

Class Assignment.   What, in your opinion, would have been the "right" action to take in each of these instances? Then, start thinking about how these situations developed. Do the senior executives at each firm know what is happening? Obviously in many instances the local people know what is happening because they were the ones who gave the instructions, but what about the more senior people at a distant location? What, if anything, would you do if you were one of those senior executives and did learn of the situation?

CASE 1–2

Five Moral Problems Encountered by Members of One MBA Class

Students in a MBA class on the ethics of management at the University of Michigan were asked to submit a written description of a moral problem they had encountered at work over the previous summer. This was a voluntary assignment. Obviously, if they had not encountered a moral problem, or if they had encountered one that they felt they could not describe without violating the implied confidence of their prior employers, they did not have to participate. Twenty-three problems were submitted. The following five were selected by members of the class for discussion at one of the subsequent meetings.

   1. *Telling lies at a market research firm.* "I was working for a market research firm in Chicago over the summer. We had an assignment to gather information from companies that used a line of industrial products. This was confidential data, on usage rate, price sensitivity, etc., and people won't fill out written questionnaires on that type of information. We had to use a telephone survey, for people will generally say much more than they intend to over the telephone if you can get them talking about the topic. We still weren't getting the information the project director wanted, so he told all of us who were doing the survey to say that we were college students, gathering the information for a term paper."

   2. *Providing gifts at a wholesale distributor.* "I was working for a company that supplied packaging materials throughout Ohio. It was just a sales job, but there was a good commission structure so that I could make a lot of money if I was successful. Packaging materials are close to a commodity. You can buy the same boxes and fillers and tape from just about anyone, at just about the same price. The suppliers tend to compete on service to the customer, and on gifts to the purchasing agent. Not all of the purchasing agents are like that, but many of them will tell you exactly what they want: a new TV for their rec room, a pair of tickets to a ball game, a new set of tires for their car. You either give them what they want, or you don't get the order."

3. *Falsifying reports at a consulting firm.* "Much of managerial consulting is not done for the purpose of helping one company compete against other companies within the same industry. Much of it is done for the purpose of helping one group within a company compete against other groups within the same company. You have one group within a company who wants to use a particular technology, or to develop a specific product, and you are hired to provide support for their project. It is clearly understood at the start what the conclusions of the report will be. If you develop some information during the study that contradicts that conclusion, you explain it to the group that arranged to have you hired, but you don't put that information in the final report to the company without the permission of the people from your group."

4. *Firing employees at a chain store.* "I was working for a discount chain store that was expanding very rapidly. I was the assistant manager for a new store that was opening in the suburbs of Richmond, Virginia. There is an awful lot of work to be done in opening a new store: you have to order the merchandise, and when it comes in you have to check it off against the right orders, put it in the right racks and on the right shelves, add the right price tags, and generally keep things organized despite the chaos of last minute construction and cleaning. I was helped by five really good people, who had been convinced to move from other stores in the chain because this was billed as a "training program" for management. We worked long hours. We got the job done. One week after the store opened, I was told to find a reason and fire three of them because "we only have room for two trainees." When I objected I was told, "Hey, there's no problem. They can go back to the jobs they came from.""

5. *Taking company property at an accounting firm.* "I spent the summer working at the office of a Big Six accounting firm in Denver. The attitude of the people in that office was 'anything goes.' Expense accounts were a joke. Nobody expected you to submit a receipt, and the result was that half of the employees cheated. People used company telephones for personal long distance calls, not just occasionally but all the time. Pencils, pens, magic markers and writing paper disappeared continually. When we left at the end of the summer to come back to school, two of the other summer interns took enough office supplies to last for the rest of the year. I never took anything, but I never told any of the senior partners either. I didn't know what I should do."

Class Assignment.   What, in your opinion, would have been the "right" action to take in each of these instances? Then, start thinking about how these situations developed. Do the senior executives at each firm know what is happening? Obviously in some instances the local people know what is happening because they were the ones who gave the instructions, but what about the more senior people at a distant location? What, if anything, would you do if you were one of those senior executives and did learn of the situation?

CASE 1–3

Green Giant's Decision to Move to Mexico

The Green Giant Company is a food products firm that specializes in canned and frozen vegetables. Started as the Minnesota Valley Canning Company in 1903, it was one of the earliest to adopt a memorable advertising character, the Jolly Green Giant who, together with his friend Little Sprout, appeared first in magazines and then on radio and eventually on television. The company's name was changed in 1950 to reflect the popularity of the advertising symbol and slogan.

Green Giant was also one of the first to adopt the new technology of freezing rather than canning vegetables, which helped greatly to preserve their taste and texture. Growth was steady during the 1950s and 60s, and the company expanded from southern Minnesota to central California where there was a much longer growing season. A large facility for freezing fresh vegetables was built at Salinas, California, about 120 miles south of San Francisco, in 1964.

The Green Giant Company was acquired, in a friendly takeover, by the Pillsbury Company of Minneapolis, Minnesota in 1978. Pillsbury produced flour, baking products and packaged cake/cookie/brownie mixes. The food industry segments of the combined firms did not overlap, so the acquisition gave Pillsbury a much broader product line with customer appeal, and a much larger output with economics of scale and scope.

In 1987, Pillsbury itself was acquired, in an unfriendly takeover, by the Grand Metropolitan Company of Great Britain. Grand Metropolitan produced alcoholic beverages and owned pubs and betting parlors in

England, Scotland, and Wales. It was said that the senior executives of that company were concerned about the decline in the consumption of alcoholic beverages as watching television at home replaced the traditional British practice of going out in the evening for a pint of beer and a game of darts at the neighborhood pub. They were determined to enter the consumer products market, and picked Pillsbury because they felt that those products, frozen fresh vegetables and packaged baking mixes, would fit other social changes, such as the growing employment of women outside the home, that were then taking place in Britain.

Pillsbury and Green Giant, together, were acquired by Grand Metropolitan when the stockholders agreed to accept a payment of $5.6 billion. Soon after the acquisition was completed, executives at Green Giant were told that they must increase the profits at that division "substantially" to help pay off debt arising from the acquisition. The executives at Green Giant were reminded that Grand Metropolitan's style of management had always been characterized as "a light but firm hand upon the throat." Failure to increase profits quickly and substantially, it was inferred, could have severe career implications.

The problem with increasing profits either quickly or substantially in the canned and frozen vegetable industry is that these products are close to commodities, with little brand recognition or consumer loyalty. Green Giant had the best-known trademark in the industry, and held the largest market share, but they still only controlled 14% of total industry sales. The remaining 86% was held by Birdseye, Del Monte, Dole, Heinz, and "house brands" produced for the various supermarket chains. Further, the per capita consumption of frozen vegetables in the United States was steady, not growing, and the canned vegetable consumption was falling as fresh produce was brought from distant nonseasonal growing regions by direct truck or even air shipment. Consequently there was little opportunity to raise sales through consumer advertising, or to increase prices through product differentiation.

It was possible, however, to decrease costs by moving from California to Mexico. Green Giant had, since 1984, operated a small freezing plant in Irapuato, Mexico. Irapuato is in central Mexico, 500 miles south of the U.S./Mexican border. The plant had been built in this area because the hot, sunny climate and dry, fertile soil produced excellent crops of cauliflower and broccoli year round, given that there was adequate water for irrigation. Green Giant had drilled a number of deep wells, and found adequate water for irrigation.

The growing, processing, and packaging of frozen vegetables for export to the U.S. from Mexico also turned out to be very inexpensive. The average wage in Irapuato was $0.65 per hour. The average wage in Salinas, California was $7.50 per hour. There were, of course, additional costs for transportation of the finished products north to the United States and for supervision of the untrained workers in Mexico, but the overall impact upon the profits of Green Giant could be very substantial and very quick if all of the California operations were moved to Mexico. It was estimated that such a move would save Green Giant $13,200 per worker per year.

In 1988, soon after the acquisition of Green Giant and Pillsbury by Grand Metropolitan, there were 1,400 workers working in the company's processing plants in the Salinas area. Salinas was a small city, almost totally dependent upon agricultural products for its livelihood. The prosperity of Silicon Valley, only 70 miles to the north in San Jose and Sunnyvale, had never reached Salinas primarily, it was said, because the population lacked the high degree of education needed for high technology electronics manufacturing.

The question, in 1988, was whether Green Giant should move all of their growing, processing, and packaging operations from Salinas to Irapuato. There were a number of factors that would impact this decision beyond the obvious savings in costs:

1. The gain of jobs and the resulting industrial development would be welcomed in Irapuato. Even though Green Giant paid only $0.65 per hour, this was still above the minimum wage for the area, set by the government at $0.55 per hour. People had lined up to get the early jobs offered at Green Giant—or Gigante Verde as the company was known locally—and it was expected that the same thing would happen if all 1,400 jobs were moved to the area. Mexican unions had tried, but failed, to organize the workers.

> Unfortunately, their employees are very happy. We can make no progress (Statement by Antonio Mosqueza, union organizer, quoted in the *San Jose News,* June 16th, 1991, p. 6)

2. The loss of the jobs, and the resulting unemployment, would be devastating to Salinas. It was expected that the economy of the area would remain agricultural, due to the excellent soil and weather conditions, but most of the jobs actually growing and harvesting the vegetables were considered to be too hard—bending and stooping under a very hot sun— for the people who had worked in the processing plants for Green Giant, many for the nearly 30 years the company had operated in Salinas.

> We helped Green Giant make their millions, and what will we be left with? Aching backs and twisted fingers. (Statement by Green Giant employee, quoted in *San Jose News,* June 16th, 1991)

3. The movement of operations from Salinas to Irapuato would have substantial environmental impacts upon the area. Central Mexico is an arid region. Water is in short supply. Green Giant has drilled wells over 450' deep to get adequate amounts of clean water for washing and blanching (lightly boiling, for about 30 seconds) the vegetables. With increased production from the move it was expected that the deep wells would dry up the 20' and 30' wells of the local population, who would then be forced to get water for cooking and washing from the river. No money was available for a municipal water system that would extend beyond the commercial center of the town. The river water could not—according to U.S. law—be used for the processing of vegetables destined for export to the United States because it is polluted by bacteria in sewage from towns that are further upstream and by pesticides that are in the runoff from the agricultural fields.

> Green Giant and the U.S government are both saying that the river water is not good enough for those of us who are so fortunate as to live in the United States but that it is plenty good enough for the Mexicans. (Verbal statement of environmental activist contacted by the case writer)

4. The movement of operations from Salinas to Irapuato would also have some social impacts upon the area. It can be assumed that Green Giant will pay taxes on their property in Mexico, though at a rate below that paid previously in California. These taxes will help to pay for needed improvements in the educational system and the physical infrastructure of the community. It can also be assumed, however, that converting about 6,000 acres of land from growing corn and beans—the local subsistence crops—to growing broccoli and cauliflower for export, will increase prices for the corn and beans and thus increase the local cost of living.

> Mexico does not have an efficient distribution system for food from one region to another. People are dependent upon what is grown locally. Water and food, of course, are the two most basic needs of life. Green Giant is going to take both of them. (Verbal statement of environmental activist contacted by the case writer)

> Green Giant is operating in a socially conscious way. We pay above the minimum wage. We provide health care for our employees. We are willing to work with the community in the construction of a water system and sewage plant. Whether you or anybody else likes it or not, Green Giant has set an example for others to follow. (Statement of Terry Thompson, vice president of Pillsbury, quoted in *San Jose News,* June 16th, 1991, p. 6).

5. The movement of operations from Salinas to Irapuato will lastly have an economic impact upon both countries. The jobs, though manual, repetitive, and dull, will be the first step in industrialization. Some of the workers will have to be selected and trained in machine repair, quality control, cost accounting, and workforce supervision. The wages, though low, will bring increases in living standards and the start of a middle class. The U.S. will benefit from the export of goods designed for that middle class, and from improved competitiveness in the world economy, as low cost labor in Mexico can be combined with capital and technology in the U.S. to counter firms from Japan and Southeastern Asia who are making extensive use of the low cost labor in parts of the Orient.

Everyone benefits from freer trade... Mexico will export more to the U.S. The U.S. will export more to Mexico. Both countries will do what they are good at doing; this is the doctrine of comparative advantage, and the standards of living in each country will rise over time. (Statement of financial economist contacted by the case writer)

The emerging global company is divorced from where it produces its goods. It has no heart, and it has no soul. It is a financial enterprise designed to maximize profits. Many of the people who inhabit it may be fine, upstanding human beings, but the organization has its own merciless logic. (Statement of labor economist, quoted in *San Jose News,* June 16th, 1991, p. 6)

Class Assignment.   Put yourself in the position of the president of Green Giant in 1988. What action would you recommend, and why? Particularly, how would you explain your recommendation to the senior executives at Grand Metropolitan to whom you report if your decision differed at all from the "substantial and quick" increase in profits which they have demanded? Lastly, do you truly believe that there is a "merciless logic" to all managerial decisions, despite the presence of "fine, upstanding human beings" within the organization?

CHAPTER 2

Managerial Ethics and Microeconomic Theory

We are concerned in this book with ethical dilemmas: decisions and actions faced by managers in which the economic performance and the social performance of the organization are in conflict. These are instances in which someone to whom the organization has some form of obligation—employees, customers, suppliers, distributors, stock-holders, or the general population in the area where the company operates—is going to be hurt or harmed in some manner, while the company is going to profit. The question is how to decide: how to find a balance between economic performance and social performance when faced by an ethical dilemma.

A balance is necessary. It is not possible, given the increasingly competitive nature of the business world, always to decide in favor of social performance. It is not possible always to keep in place surplus employees following a merger. It is not possible always to retain obsolete distributors when the economics of the industry have changed. It is not possible always to delay building a dam for power generation because it will destroy recreational opportunities for local residents.

On the other side, however, it is not possible always to decide in favor of economic performance. We can all picture a manager murmuring something about a need to be tough in the three instances above and then firing the surplus employees, replacing the obsolete distributors, and building the new dam. But that was the reason for listing the other ethical dilemmas faced by recent graduates of business schools. Is it possible always to disregard older people, living on fixed incomes, when making a product or pricing decision? Is it possible always to disregard potential customers, and an obligation to be truthful to them, when designing an advertising program? Is it possible always to disregard unpleasant if not hazardous working conditions for production employees in planning capital improvements at a manufacturing plant? If these illustrations at the operating level are not enough, we can move on to the more dramatic examples at the corporate or strategic level that were listed briefly in the previous chapter. Is it right to bribe foreign political leaders to ensure the purchase of the company's products? Is it right to overbill the Defense Department for large, nonessential expenditures to increase the company's profits? Is it right to make fictitious deposits at banks to earn $8 million of interest? Is it right to substitute artificial flavors and sweeteners for natural apple juice in a drink prepared for babies?

I think that we can all agree, in some of the instances above, that "No, it is not right." At some point along that vector of examples, listed generally in a ranking of increasing moral severity, people's opinions change from, "Yes, that seems to be all right" to "No, that is definitely wrong." It is a question of where to draw the line. Another way of expressing that same thought is to say that it is a question of how to balance the economic versus the social performance of the firm.

There are three forms of analysis that can help in drawing the line, that can assist in reaching a decision on the proper balance between economic and social performance. These forms of analysis are economic, based upon impersonal market forces; legal, based upon impersonal social forces; and philosophical, based upon personal principles and values. In this chapter we are going to look at economic analysis, based upon impersonal market forces.

THE MORAL CONTENT OF MICROECONOMIC THEORY

Economic analysis as a means of finding the proper or moral balance between the economic and social performance of a business firm may seem to you to be an anomaly, an impossibility. That, however, is not accurate; there is a definite moral content to microeconomic theory.

For many persons, the concept of morality in microeconomics—the theory of the firm—is a contradiction in terms. They learned the theory as a logical and mathematical approach to markets and prices and production, devoid of moral substance. As a result of this education, most noneconomists, and perhaps a few economists as well, appear to focus almost entirely on profit maximization. They view the theory as descriptive, designed to rationalize the behavior of business managers, and believe that such single-minded pursuit of profit automatically excludes any consideration of environmental health, worker safety, consumer interests, or other "side issues."

Overconcentration on profits doubtless has resulted in these and other problems within our society, but that is neither a consequence nor a corollary of microeconomic theory. Microeconomic theory, in its more complete form, addresses these issues and includes ethical as well as economic precepts.

Microeconomic theory in its complete form is more a normative theory of society than a descriptive theory of the firm. Profit maximization is a part of the theory, but it is only a part, and certainly not the central focus, though it must be admitted, and this adds to the lack of under-standing, that techniques for profit maximization occupy a central portion of the curriculum at many schools of business administration.

The central focus of the larger theory of society is the efficient utilization of resources to satisfy consumer wants and needs. At economic equilibrium—and an essential element in reaching equilibrium through-out the entire economic system is the effort by business managers to balance marginal increases in revenues against marginal increases in costs, which automatically results in optimal profits for the firm within market and resource constraints—it is theoretically possible to achieve Pareto Optimality.

Pareto Optimality refers to a condition in which the scarce resources of society are being used so efficiently by the producing firms, and the goods and services are being distributed so effectively by the competi-tive markets, that it would be impossible to make any single person better off without harming some other person. Remember this phrase: "It would be impossible to make any single person better off without making some other person worse off." This is the ethical substance of microeconomic theory encapsulated in Pareto Optimality: produce the maximum economic benefits for society, recognizing the full personal and social costs of that production, and then broaden the receipt of those benefits if necessary by political, not economic, actions.

Pareto Optimality provides the ethical content of microeconomic theory. Without this concept of maximum social benefit at minimal social cost, the theory deteriorates into a simple prescription for individual gain and corporate profit. With this concept, the theory becomes a means of achieving a social goal: maximum numbers of goods and services produced at minimum costs.

The theory requires that every business manager attempt to optimize profits. Consequently the decision rule that a microeconomist would propose for finding the proper balance between the economic and social performance of a business firm would be to always be truthful, honor-able (i.e., observe contracts), and competitive, and always decide for the greater economic return. The question of this chapter is: Can we use this decision rule when faced with an ethical dilemma?

For many microeconomists, the concept of Pareto Optimality excludes any need to consider ethical dilemmas in management. This view is very direct and can be summarized very simply. "Ethics are not rele-vant in business, beyond the normal standards not to lie, cheat, or steal. All that is necessary is to maintain price-competitive markets and recog-nize the full costs of production in those prices, and then the market system will ensure that scarce resources are used to optimally satisfy consumer needs. A firm that is optimally satisfying consumer needs, to the limit of the available resources, is operating most efficiently and most profitably. Consequently, business managers should act to maximize profits, while following legal requirements of nonconclusion and equal opportunity and adhering to personal standards of truthfulness and honesty. Profit maximization leads automatically from the satisfaction of individual consumer wants to the generation of maximum social benefits. Profit maximization is the only moral standard needed for management."

Is this summary an overstatement of the microeconomic view of ethics and management? Probably not. The belief that profit maximization leads inexorably to the well-being of society is a central tenet of economic theory and has been stated very succinctly and very clearly by both James McKie of the Brookings Institution and Milton Friedman of the University of Chicago:

> The primary goal and motivating force for business organizations is profit. The firm attempts to make as large a profit as it can, thereby maintaining its efficiency and taking advantage of available opportunities to innovate and contribute to growth. Profits are kept to reasonable or appropriate levels by market competition, which leads the firm pursuing its own self-interest to an end that is not part of its conscious intention: enhancement of the public welfare.[1]

* * * * *

> The view has been gaining widespread acceptance that corporate officials. . . . have a "social responsibility" that goes beyond serving the interest of their stockholders or their members. This view shows a fundamental misconception of the character and nature of a free economy. In such an economy, there is one and only one social responsibility of business—to use its resources and engage in activities designed to increase its profits, so long as it stays within the rules of the game, which is to say, engages in open and free competition, without deception or fraud. . . . Few trends could so thoroughly undermine the very foundations of our free society as the acceptance by corporate officials of a social responsibility other than to make as much money for their stockholders as possible.[2]

The statement by Milton Friedman was expanded in an article, "The Social Responsibility of Business Is to Increase Its Profits,"[3] which often is assigned for students at business schools in classes on business economics or business and society. It is a frustrating article to read and then to discuss in class because it never makes clear the theoretical basis of Pareto Optimality; Professor Friedman assumed that readers would recognize and understand that basis of his contention.

THE MORAL PROBLEMS IN MICROECONOMIC THEORY

What is your opinion? Can we accept the microeconomic premise that profit optimization leads directly to maximum social benefits? The response of people trained in other disciplines is often much more pragmatic than theoretical, and it too can be summarized very simply: "Yes, we know the theory, but look at where the blind pursuit of profit has led us: foreign bribes, environmental problems, unsafe products, closed plants, and injured workers. We need something more than profit to measure our obligations to society." This view, I think, has been most sensibly expressed by Manuel Velasquez of the University of Santa Clara:

> ...some have argued that in perfectly competitive free markets the pursuit of profit will by itself ensure that the members of society are served in the most socially beneficial ways. For, in order to be profitable each firm has to produce only what the members of society want and has to do this by the most efficient means available. The members of society will benefit most, then, if managers do not impose their own values on a business but instead devote themselves to the single-minded pursuit of profit, and thereby devote themselves to producing efficiently what the members of society themselves value.

> Arguments of this sort conceal a number of assumptions. . . . First, most industrial markets are not "perfectly competitive" as the argument assumes, and to the extent that firms do not have to compete they can maximize profits in spite of inefficient production. Second, the argument assumes that any steps taken to increase profits will necessarily be socially beneficial, when in fact several ways of increasing profits actually injure society: allowing harmful pollution to go uncontrolled, deceptive advertising, concealing product hazards, fraud, bribery, tax evasion, price-fixing, and so on. Third, the argument assumes that by producing whatever the buying public wants (or values) firms are producing what all the members of society want, when in fact the wants of large segments of society (the poor and the disadvantaged) are not necessarily met because they cannot participate fully in the marketplace. . . . [4]

This pragmatic response, which can obviously be supported by many examples within our society, is not compelling to most economists. They believe that the issues cited—the lack of competitive markets, the presence of injurious practices, and the exclusion of some segments of society—are part of economic theory and would be prevented by its strict application. How would they be prevented? Here, it is necessary to provide an explanation of the extensive structure of economic theory and of the logical interrelationships that exist among the components in that structure: the individual consumers, product markets, producing firms, factor markets, factor owners, and public institutions. (The "factors" are the scarce resources of labor, capital, and material used in the production of goods and services.) Doubtless an explanation of this structure and these interrelationships will be dull for those with a good grasp of microeconomic theory, and trying for all others, but this explanation is necessary to deal with the ethical problems in the theory on a meaningful basis. If you truly are bored with microeconomic theory and willing to accept the rationality of the structure, skip ahead to page (page 44) and dive directly into the ethical claims of the theory.

THE BASIC STRUCTURE OF MICROECONOMIC THEORY

Microeconomic theory is complex. Perhaps, to make this brief explanation more comprehensible, it would be well to start with an overall summary. The focus of the theory, as stated previously, is the efficient utilization of scarce resources to maximize the production of wanted goods and services. The mechanism of the theory is the market structure: each firm is located between a "factor" market for the input factors of production (labor, material, and capital) and a "product" market for the output goods and services. The demand for each good or service is aggregated from the preference functions of individual consumers, who act to maximize their satisfactions from a limited mix of products. The supply of each good or service is aggregated from the production schedules of individual firms, which act to balance their marginal revenues and marginal costs at a limited level of capacity.

The production of goods and services creates derived demands for the input factors of labor, material, and capital. These factors are substitutable—can be interchanged—so the derived demands vary with the costs. These costs, of course, reflect the constrained supplies in the different factor markets. A firm attempting to minimize costs and maximize revenues will therefore use the most available resources to produce the most needed products, generating not only the greatest profits for itself but the greatest benefits for society. The components of the theory, and the relationships among these components, which together produce corporate profits and social benefits, may be more understandable in graphic form, as shown in Exhibit 2–1.

Now it is necessary to work through the theory in somewhat greater detail to indicate the inclusion of ethical concepts and to be able to discuss the ethical problems that are integral with it.

Individual Consumers

Each consumer has a slightly different set of preferences for the various goods and services that are available, and these preferences can be expressed as "utilities," or quantitative measures of the usefulness of a given product or service to a specific customer. The "marginal utility," or extra usefulness, of one additional unit of that product or service to that customer tends to decline, for eventually the person will have a surfeit of the good.

The price that the person is willing to pay for the good also declines along with the marginal utility or degree of surfeit. Price relative to the number of units that will be purchased by a given person at a given time forms the individual demand curve (see Exhibit 2–2).

Exhibit 2–1

Graphic Summary of Microeconomic Theory

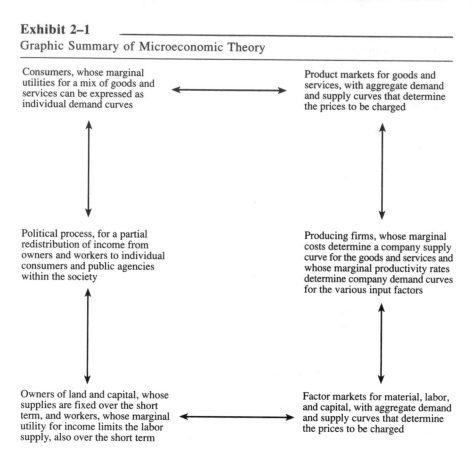

Consumers, whose marginal utilities for a mix of goods and services can be expressed as individual demand curves

Product markets for goods and services, with aggregate demand and supply curves that determine the prices to be charged

Political process, for a partial redistribution of income from owners and workers to individual consumers and public agencies within the society

Producing firms, whose marginal costs determine a company supply curve for the goods and services and whose marginal productivity rates determine company demand curves for the various input factors

Owners of land and capital, whose supplies are fixed over the short term, and workers, whose marginal utility for income limits the labor supply, also over the short term

Factor markets for material, labor, and capital, with aggregate demand and supply curves that determine the prices to be charged

Price can also be used to compare the relative usefulness of different goods and services to an individual. It can be expected that a person selecting a mix of products will choose an assortment of goods and services such that marginal utility per monetary unit would be equal for all the items at a given level of spending for this individual. Each good would be demanded up to the point where the marginal utility per dollar would be exactly the same as the marginal utility per dollar for any other good. If a customer had a higher marginal utility relative to price for any particular good, he or she would doubtless substitute more of that good for some of the others to achieve a better balance among his or her preferences. The final balance or mix, where the marginal utilities per monetary unit are equal for all products and services, can be termed the point of equilibrium for that customer.

The concept of consumer equilibrium is an important element in the structure of the economic condition termed Pareto Optimality. A customer with balanced marginal utilities per monetary unit for all available

Exhibit 2–2
Personal Demand Curve

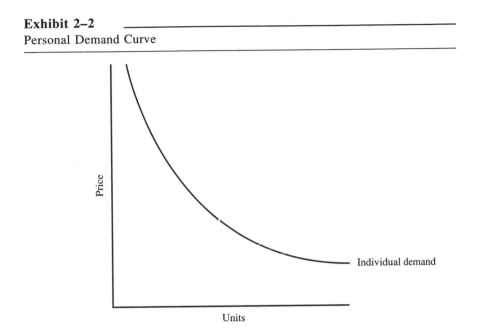

goods and services cannot be made better off at his or her level of spending, according to his or her standards of preference. The customer may buy hamburgers, french fries, and beer, and we may think that he or she should be buying fish, fresh vegetables, and fruit, but that person is satisfying his or her standards, not our own, and they are being satisfied up to the limits of his or her ceiling on expenditures. Consequently, that person cannot be made better off without an increase in disposable income.

Now, let us look at the determination of the level of disposable income in microeconomic theory. This is more complex than the determination of the mix of desired purchases, but the logical structure can be followed through the product markets, the producing firms, the factor markets, the private owners of those factors, and the public processes for redistribution of factor income.

Product Markets

A product market consists of all the customers for a given good or service, together with all the producing firms that supply that good or service. The individual demand curves of all the customers can be aggregated to form a market demand curve. The market demand curve reflects the total demand for a good or service, relative to price. If price is the vertical axis and demand the horizontal axis, the market demand curve will generally slope downward and towards the right, indicating increased potential purchases at the lower price levels.

Crossing this market demand curve is a market supply curve that portrays the total available supply, again relative to price. The market supply curve generally slopes upward and towards the right, for the higher the price, the more units in total most companies can be expected to manufacture, until they reach a short-term limit of capacity. The market price, of course, is set at the intersection of the curves representing aggregate demand and aggregate supply (see Exhibit 2–3).

Producing Firms

The aggregate supply curve, the "other half" of each product market, is formed by adding together the individual supply curves of all the producers. These individual supply curves are generated by the cost structures of the producing firms at different levels of production, while the actual level of production is determined by a comparison of "marginal revenues" and "marginal costs."

The marginal revenue of a producing firm is the extra revenue that the firm would receive by selling one additional unit of the good or service. To sell that additional unit in a fully price-competitive market, it is necessary to move down the aggregate demand curve to a slightly lower price level. To sell that additional unit in a non-price-competitive market, it is necessary to spend greater amounts on advertising and promotion to differentiate the product from those manufactured by other firms. Under

Exhibit 2–3

Market Demand and Supply Curve

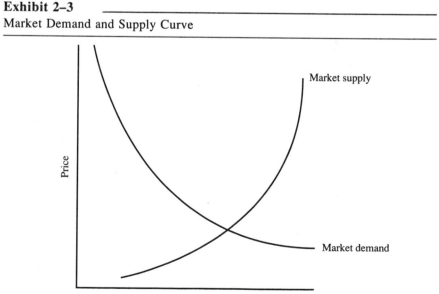

either alternative, the marginal revenue from selling the last unit will be less than the average revenue from selling all other units. Marginal revenues inevitably decrease with volume.

The marginal cost of the producing firm is the obverse of the marginal revenue. Marginal cost is the extra expense that the firm would incur by producing one additional unit of the product or service. Marginal costs initially decline with volume due to economies of scale and learning curve effects, but they eventually rise due to diminishing returns as the physical capacity of the plant is approached. The rising portion of the marginal cost curve forms the supply curve of the firm; it represents the number of units that the firm should produce and supply to the market at each price level (see Exhibit 2–4)

The producing firm achieves equilibrium when marginal costs are equal to marginal revenues. At the intersection of the marginal cost and marginal revenue curves, the profits of the firm are maximized. The firm can increase profits only by improving its technology; this would change the marginal costs and consequently the supply curve. However, over the long term, all firms would adopt the new technology and achieve the same cost structure. Production equilibrium would be reestablished at the new intersections of the marginal cost and marginal revenue curves for all firms within the industry.

All the costs of production have to be included in computing the marginal cost curve for a firm. This is the second of the ethical constructs in microeconomic theory, along with the individual selection of goods

Exhibit 2–4

Marginal Cost Curve

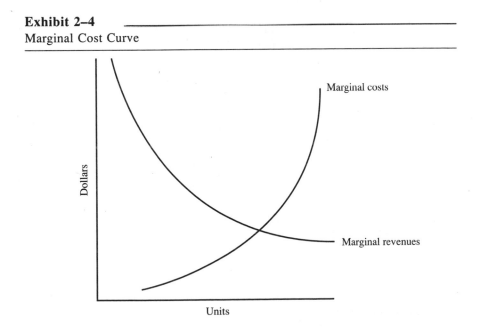

and services according to private preference standards, or "utilities." The internal personal costs (e.g., hazardous working conditions) and the external social costs (e.g., harmful environmental discharges) have to be computed, so that customers pay the full costs of production. The technology, of course, can be changed to improve working conditions and reduce environmental discharges, and this should be done to bring marginal costs down to marginal revenues at a new, nonhazardous and nonpolluting equilibrium, but it is an essential element in microeconomic theory that product-market prices reflect the *full* costs of production.

Factor Markets

The technology of the producing firm determines the maximum output of goods and services that can be achieved for a given mix of input factors. The input factors of production are land (an apparently obsolete term that instead refers to all of the basic raw materials), labor, and capital. Charges for the input factors are rents for the land and other basic resources, wages for the labor, and interest for the capital. These charges are interdependent because the factors are interrelated; that is, one factor may be substituted for others in the production function.

The relationships among these input factors, and the amount of one that would have to be used to substitute for another, are determined by the technology of the production function and by the "marginal productivity" of each factor for a given technology. The marginal productivity of a factor of production is the additional output generated by adding one more unit of that factor while keeping all others constant. For example, it would be possible to add one additional worker to a production line without changing the capital investments in the line or the material components of the product. There should then be an increase in the physical output of that production line, and that increase, measured in units or portions of units, would be the marginal productivity of that worker. To maximize profits, a company should increase the use of each factor of production until the value of its marginal product (the increase in unit output, or productivity, times the price of those units) equals the cost of the input factor.

Factor Owners

The aggregate demand for each factor of production is equal to the proportion of that factor used in the production function of each firm times the output of those functions supplied to meet the product market demand. The demand for each factor of production is therefore "derived" from the primary markets for goods and services.

The aggregate supply of each factor of production, however, is limited. Over the long term, stocks of the basic materials may be expanded by bringing into production marginal agricultural lands, oilfields, and ore mines, while the reserves of investment capital may be increased by raising the rate of capital formation. Over the short term, however, the supply amounts are fixed. Aggregate supplies of labor are also limited, though for a different cause: each worker has a marginal utility for income that decreases and becomes negative as his or her desire for greater leisure exceeds his or her preference for further work. This negative utility function creates a "backward sloping" supply curve for labor and sharply limits the amounts available at the higher wage rates (see Exhibit 2–5).

The price system in the different factor markets, therefore, ensures that the limited factors of production will be used in the most economically effective manner to produce the goods and services to be sold in the product markets, and that the rents, wages, and interest paid for these factors will reflect both the productivity of the factor and the derived demand of the goods.

Political Processes

The owners of the factors of production, within a capitalistic society, are also the customers for the products and services generated by the production functions at the various firms. The owners receive the rents, the wages, and the interest payments for the use of their resources and then purchase the goods and services they want, following their personal preferences or utilities.

Exhibit 2–5
Factor Supply Curves

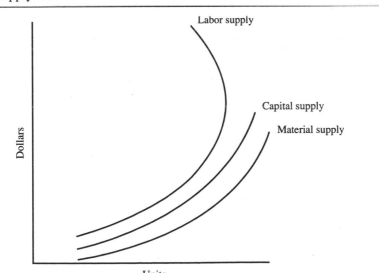

There is a political process for the redistribution of the rents, wages, and interest payments, through both tax provisions and welfare allocations, so that no individual or group is unable to participate in the product markets for the various goods and services. This political process is the third ethical construct in microeconomic theory. It ensures that the distribution of the revenues for material, capital, and labor will be "equitable," following a democratically determined definition of equity.

THE MORAL CLAIMS OF MICROECONOMIC THEORY

Now that there is a common understanding of the basic structure of microeconomic theory, or the logical system of relationships among individual customers, product markets, producing firms, factor markets, resource owners, and political processes, it is possible to look at the claims of that theory relative to the social welfare. There are five explicit assertions:

1. The price mechanisms of the factor markets allocate the scarce resources of society to their most effective uses. The marginal productivity of each factor together with the cost (reflecting supply versus demand) determines the relative usage of the factors by the producing firms. At factor equilibrium, it would be impossible to expand total production without an increase in resource supply.

2. The production functions of the producing firms convert the limited input factors into wanted output goods and services by the most effective methods (process technologies) and at the most efficient rates (output amounts). A firm's technology and capacity are long-term decisions, while the operating rate is a short-term choice, but all are based upon the balance between marginal revenues and marginal costs. Internal personal harms and external social damages are included in the marginal costs. At process equilibrium, it would be impossible to convert resources into products more efficiently and with less personal harm or social damage without an advance in technology.

3. The price mechanisms of the product markets distribute the wanted goods and services of society to their most effective uses. The marginal utilities of each customer together with the prices (again reflecting supply versus demand) for the various products determine the relative consumption of the goods and services. At market equilibrium, it would be impossible to improve consumer satisfaction without an increase in personal income.

4. The political processes of the national society determine the personal income of each consumer through democratic means. The income may be distributed according to ownership of the factors of production, or according to an individual's need, effort, contribution, or competence. Distribution of the benefits of the economic system is a political, not an economic, process.

5. The economic system, provided the managers of the producing firms act to maximize profits, the customers for the goods and services act to maximize satisfactions, and the owners of the resources act to maximize revenues, will operate as efficiently as possible, producing the greatest output of wanted goods and services for the least input of scarce labor, capital, and material. If the revenues to the owners of the factors of production are equitably redistributed to the customers of the producing firms through a democratic decision process, it would be impossible to improve the life of any member of the system without harming the life of another member, because the system would have reached Pareto Optimality. Consequently, the social responsibility of the managers of the producing firms is to maximize profits and leave the redistribution of economic benefits to the political process.

PRAGMATIC OBJECTIONS TO MICROECONOMIC THEORY

The usual objections to microeconomic theory are pragmatic in nature, based upon very obvious problems in our national society, and they generally include the three issues discussed by Professor Velasquez in the statement quoted earlier in this chapter:

1. The exclusion of segments of society. It is alleged that the minorities and the poor, because they lack ownership of any of the factors of production beyond their unskilled labor, receive inadequate income to participate in the product markets and consequently cannot maximize their own satisfactions in any meaningful way. The microeconomic response is quite obvious. "We grant you that this happens, but it is the fault of the political process and not of the economic system. You develop logically attractive political decision rules for the more equitable division of the benefits, and we will work to economically maximize the production of those benefits within market and resource constraints."

2. The presence of injurious practices. It is also alleged that managers of productive firms, because of an excessive concern with maximizing profits, have permitted or even encouraged some practices that are injurious to some members of society, through workplace dangers or environmental pollution, or that are destructive to the market system, through purchase bribes or employment discrimination. Here, the response of most economists would be that these problems occur, but that they would not occur under the strict application of the theory. Let us look at a number of specific problems and the theoretical solutions:

Purchase Bribes.   Personal payments to influence purchase decisions are evidently common overseas, and not unknown within the United States. In an efficient market, however, bribes would be futile; they would raise the cost function by an amount equivalent to the payment, so that nonbribing competitors would have an obvious price advantage. The microeconomic response is obvious: Insist that purchase decisions be open and subject to public comparison of the bids, to ensure the selection of the lowest-priced proposal to supply needed goods and services. The lowest-priced proposal would necessarily come from a nonbribing competitor.

Process Pollutants.   Many industrial processes result in toxic residues and inert materials as by-products, which are now either discharged as air or water pollutants or buried as liquid or solid wastes. The toxic by-products have an obvious social cost, both immediate and long term. The microeconomic response has been clearly stated many times: companies should recognize these costs that are external to the productive process and include them in the pricing function. It might be expected, were these external costs accurately computed, that investments in proper disposal equipment would become clearly beneficial for the firm, or if they were fully included in the price, the product would become overly expensive for the customer to buy. Under either alternative, the amount of pollution would be substantially reduced.

Workplace Hazards.   It would appear that many of the mechanical hazards of industrial processing have been eliminated. Forty years of state and federal labor laws have removed most of the unprotected belts, open gearing, and nonshielded presses. Chemical risks still remain, however, and psychological problems will probably always be a part of mass manufacturing, due to the repetitive nature of the tasks and the time constraints of the process: The microeconomic response to workplace hazards is similar to that for process pollutants: the nonfactor costs of production should be computed and added to the price. Certainly, if the market is to operate efficiently to allocate resources within the society, customers have to pay the full costs of production, not partial costs subsidized by the physical or mental health of the workers.

Product Dangers.   The press has recently reported numerous instances of unsafe products, particularly in the automobile industry. Gas tanks poorly located, radial tires poorly fabricated, and automatic transmissions poorly designed have all been mentioned, together with such nonautomotive products as hair dryers (containing asbestos), teddy bears (containing sharp objects), and packaged foods (containing nonnutrients). I think it safe to assume that the microeconomic response would be that a product offered for sale within a competitive market should perform the function for which it was designed, and that many of the reported failures and hazards come from decisions to differentiate products in slight or artificial ways to avoid the discipline of price competition. Whatever the cause of product failures and hazards, the costs of improper design are now being charged back against the manufacturing firms through liability suits and jury awards, and it can be assumed that product safety will soon be improved as a result of objective economic analysis.

Minority Employment.   Racial or sexual discrimination in employment, in an efficient labor market, would be self-defeating; a workforce limited to young or middle-aged white males would raise the cost of labor in the productive function and provide the nondiscriminating employer with a cost advantage. It is assumed, in economic analysis, that all groups are equal in performance capabilities. Training might be needed to justify that assumption, but the microeconomic response would be that training to correct social injustices should be provided as a public investment. Cost-benefit analysis would assuredly show an economic return on that investment, as well as a social gain.

3. The absence of competitive markets. Lastly, it is often claimed that the product markets for consumer goods and services are not price competitive because of oligopolistic practices among the producing firms serving those markets. Companies have become much larger recently, doubtless due to economies of scale in production and distribution, while products have become more "differentiated," marked by only slight or imagined distinctions in performance and design but supported by large-scale advertising. The dominance of large firms in each market, and the inability of customers to judge the relative worth of products in those markets, is said to lead toward "administered" rather than competitive prices. Administered pricing, where the price level is set by the company to provide a set return above costs without reference to either supply or demand, of course destroys the efficiency of the market. The economic response, however, is very simple. "Oh, we grant you that market structures are not truly competitive, and that market processes are not actually efficient under current conditions. However, no one is advocating limited competition or inadequate information. Public policy changes to restrict competitor size and to ensure consumer information are needed to reestablish the discipline of the market."

THEORETIC OBJECTIONS TO MICROECONOMIC THEORY

Microeconomic theory is awesomely complete. There are few operating decisions in business to which it could not be applied—from hiring workers, purchasing supplies, and borrowing money to selecting technologies, establishing capacities, and setting prices. Likewise, there are few ethical problems to which microeconomic theory is not applicable, whether purchase bribes, process pollutants, workplace hazards, product dangers, or racial discrimination. It is very difficult to say, "Here is a managerial decision or action with definite ethical implications that is not included in the theory."

Microeconomic theory is also enviably unified. All the managerial decisions and actions work together, through a system of explicit relationships, to create a socially desirable goal: maximum output of the wanted goods and services at a minimum input of the scarce material, capital, and labor. It is very difficult to say, "Here is a managerial decision or action following microeconomic theory that does not lead to a socially beneficial outcome."

Where does this discussion lead us? Are we forced to accept microeconomic theory as an ethical system of belief for business management because of the complete and unified nature of the paradigm? Should we always act to maximize profits, as long as we are truthful, honest, and competitive, and use the concept of Pareto Optimality as the substitute for our ethical concerns? Or, is there a theoretic problem with that paradigm?

Most non-economists are intuitively distressed by the proposal that business managers have no moral responsibilities to other members of society, outside of fiduciary duties to a small circle of owners, and that managers also are governed by no moral requirements of behavior beyond adhering to personal standards of honesty and truthfulness, observing legal statutes for contracts and against collusion, and computing accurate costs for personal harms and social dangers. Why is this distressing, and what are the arguments against the microeconomic model that can be expressed on a theoretic rather than a pragmatic or intuitive basis? There are two major arguments; one pertains to the assumptions about human nature and the second centers on the assumptions about human worth that are part of microeconomic theory.

1. Assumptions about the nature of human beings. The microeconomic model is utilitarian (see Chapter 4 for a definition of utilitarianism, a philosophic system that has often been roughly translated as "the greatest good for the greatest number"). It takes the position that the ultimate end is the greatest general good, and it defines that good as the maximum benefits of consumer products and services at the minimum costs of labor, capital, and material. The problem, as with all utilitarian theories, is that the distribution of the benefits and the imposition of the costs may be unjust. Consequently, it is necessary to add a political process to the economic paradigm to ensure justice in the distribution of benefits and the imposition of costs.

But, "justice" is defined in the theory as a democratically determined pattern of distribution and imposition; this pattern does not follow a rule such as, to each person equally, or to each according to his or her need, to his or her effort, to his or her contribution, to his or her competence, or even to his or her ownership of the factors of production. Instead, the pattern varies with the collective opinions of the members of society. This requires all members of society to be actively concerned with the charitable distribution of social benefits and sensitive imposition of social costs at the same time as they are actively concerned with the personal maximization of material goods and services in the product markets and of financial wages, rents, and interest payments in the factor markets.

I think that we can safely say that human nature exhibits both selfish and generous traits, and we can doubtless go further and accept that human beings can perform selfish and then generous acts alternately, but it would seem an extreme assumption to believe that people can concurrently be generously attentive to others in all political decisions and selfishly attentive to themselves in all economic activities, and never confuse the two roles. The microeconomic model would appear to be based upon an exceedingly complex and unlikely view of the nature of human beings.

2. Assumptions about the value of human beings. The microeconomic model is impersonal, for it requires that everyone be treated as a means to an end and not as an end in himself or herself. Customers for goods and services are people who maximize material satisfactions as a means of determining product demand curves. Owners of land, capital, and labor are people who maximize financial revenues as a means of determining factor-supply curves. Company managers are people who maximize corporate profits as a means of balancing market demand and factor supply. No one acts as an individual human being, pursuing personal goals worthy of consideration and respect.

This denial of worth can be seen particularly clearly in the position of the manager of the firm, who must act solely as an agent for the financial interests of the stockholders. What does this do to self-esteem and to self-respect? How can people live worthwhile lives when always being treated as a means to other people's ends—or, perhaps even worse, when always treating others as means to their own ends—even though the society as an economic system may have achieved Pareto Optimality? The microeconomic model would ap-pear to be based upon an exceedingly low view of the worth of human beings.

Where does this discussion of managerial ethics and microeconomic theory lead us? There would seem to be two major conclusions. If we look at microeconomic theory as a structured pattern of relationships explaining the optimal uses of scarce material, capital, and labor to produce the optimal numbers of consumer goods and services, then it is a logically complete and intellectually satisfying view of the world. But, if we look at microeconomic theory as an ethical system of belief, explaining our responsibility to others within the company and within the society—to employees, customers, suppliers, distributors, and residents of the local area—then it simply falls apart because of the unlikely assumptions about human nature and human worth. We are going to have to look elsewhere for a means of reaching decisions when confronted with an ethical dilemma, with a conflict between the economic performance and the social performance of a business firm. We are going to have to look either to the rule of law or to the doctrines of normative philosophy to determine what is "right" and "just" and "proper."

Footnotes

1. James McKie, "Changing Views," in *Social Responsibility and the Business Predicament* (Washington, D.C.: Brookings Institution, 1974), p. 19.

2. Milton Friedman, *Capitalism and Freedom* (Chicago: University of Chicago Press, 1962), p. 133.

3. *New York Times Magazine,* September 13, 1970, p. 32f.

4. Manuel Velasquez, *Business Ethics: Concepts and Cases* (New York: Prentice-Hall, 1982), pp. 17–18.

CASE 2–1

When Is It Permissible to Tell a Lie?

Lying can be defined as making a statement that the speaker knows to be false, with the intention of misleading other people. Knowledge and intention are both central to the concept of a lie. The speaker must know the relative truth or falsity of the assertion, and must intend to deceive, for most of us to brand the statement as a lie. Yet, some deliberately deceptive statements are still considered to be "O.K." by people active in business. Which of the following deliberately deceptive statements do you consider to be permissible, given the circumstances in which they occur:

1. *You are an export manager for a U.S. steel company* that provides heavy beams and plates prefabricated for large construction projects. You have a $20 million order for a project in a South American country. You need just one last approval from a government official During a verbal discussion in that person's office he requests a $20,000 bribe. You are surprised because the official policy in his country has changed recently, under a reformist regime, and bribes are now strongly forbidden. You say that it is against U.S. law and company rules for you to make that payment. He shrugs slightly, and says "Fine, we will give the order to the Japanese." It happens that you have a battery-powered tape recorder in your briefcase. You use it to dictate memos after meetings such as this one. It has not been turned on, but of course the government official does not know that. Is it permissible for you to open your briefcase, take out the tape recorder, show it to the official, and say, "It is a policy of our company to record all conversations with government officials in Central and South America. Do you wish this tape to be given to the minister in charge of your agency, or do you wish to sign the necessary papers for our import permit?" (Note: I am indebted to Prof. Joanne Ciulla of the University of Richmond for this true example.)

2. *You are a senior manager at a large chemical company.* You have just learned that some highly toxic by-products at one of your plants have been improperly dumped in steel drums. Fortunately the Director of Safety at your company learned about this situation, and was able to retrieve the barrels before "too much" leakage had occurred. She and others have assured you that there is no danger to public health, but local newspapers have heard of the situation and want to interview you. The corporate attorney has warned you that despite the prompt action the company doubtless will be sued and that you should not, under any circumstance, admit liability. Is it proper for you to say that there was no leakage, and consequently no danger?

3. *You are a member of the human resources staff* at a large consumer products firm. You have completed the annual series of interviews at colleges and universities, have arranged "flybacks" for a selected number of the people who were interviewed, have summarized the comments of the managers who met the candidates during their plant visits, and have prioritized them according to those comments. You know that job offers have been made to the top five persons on that list. You also know that it is traditional, when a job offer is made by your company, for the candidate to be given two weeks in which to decide, and to be asked to treat the offer as confidential until he or she decides formally whether to accept or reject the offer. Lastly, you know that people who don't quite make the first cut-off tend to become defensive, if they hear of it, and quickly accept another offer. Now, the person who stands number seven on the list calls you, and asks whether the decision has been made. Is it permissible for you to say that the final decision is still pending, but that you are certain that the person will hear something, either positively or negatively, within two weeks?

4. *You are an assistant in the strategic planning department at a large manufacturing firm.* One of the responsibilities of your department is to gather information about the production processes, cost structures, marketing policies, and research budgets of your competitors. Much of this information can be taken from published sources such as annual reports, local newspapers, trade journals, and business magazines. The really "good stuff", however, is said to be obtained most easily by talking to mid-level employees of the targeted company. One way is to simply call them. A strategic planner who has done this frequently says, "People are generally proud of what they have accomplished, and they like to be asked. I call someone in marketing, for example, say that we are doing some bench marking (comparing our operations to those of well regarded competitors) and ask a few questions. Inevitably they tell me much, much more than they should." Another way is to invite them to a job interview, and the same strategic planner says, "You don't have to lie to them. You don't have to mislead them. You don't even have to actually invite them to an interview. All you have to do is to call and say that your company has a job opening—it inevitably does—and ask if they are interested. Everybody wants to advance their own careers, so they are interested. Then, you ask about their most recent accomplishments, and you generally get the information you want over the telephone. Before you hang up you say that you are very glad that you called, that they do sound like the sort of person that your company needs in production or marketing or whatever, and that you'll get back to them as soon as the position is confirmed in the next budget. Of course, you never do get back to them." Is it permissible to make those calls?

Class Assignment.   Decide which of these actions are "right" and which are "wrong." Follow your own opinion, but be prepared to support that opinion. Then, start thinking about how these situations developed. Do the senior executives at each firm know what is happening? What, if anything, would you do if you were one of the senior executives and did know of the situation?

CASE 2–2

Financial Compensation for the Victims of Bhopal

On December 3, 1984, some 2,000 people were killed and 200,000 were injured when a cloud of poisonous methyl isocyanate gas was accidentally released from the Union Carbide Company plant in Bhopal, India. The methyl isocyanate was used to manufacture Sevin, a plant pesticide that was distributed widely throughout India for use on that country's corn, rice, soybean, cotton, and alfalfa crops. It was said that the use of Sevin increased the harvest of the food crops by over 10 percent, enough to feed 70 million people.

The accident apparently occurred when between 120 and 240 gallons of water were introduced into a storage tank containing 90,000 pounds of methyl isocyanate. It is not known how or why the water was introduced into the tank. Operator inattention, employee sabotage, and corporate error have all been mentioned. It is not even known for certain that water in the tank was the direct cause of the tragedy, though that view does have some scientific validity and is supported by the company.

Following the accident, seven engineers and scientists were sent from the Union Carbide headquarters in Connecticut to the plant site at Bhopal to assist in the safe disposal of the remaining methyl isocyanate within the damaged tank, and to investigate the reasons for the horrendous accident. They were not permitted to interview the operators of the Sevin process or to inspect the remains of the methyl isocyanate tank and related piping. They were permitted to obtain samples of the residues from the nearly ruptured tank. Through experimentation they were able to replicate reactions that led to residues with the same chemical properties in the same proportions. The following account, therefore is a hypotheses for the tragedy, not a proven and accepted series of events.

The storage tank for methyl isocyanate also contained approximately 3,000 pounds of chloroform, according to this view. Chloroform was used as a solvent in the manufacture of the methyl isocyanate.The two chemicals should have been separated before storage, but that had not been done for some time in the operating process at Bhopal.

The water in the tank reacted exothermically (producing heat) with the chloroform, generating chlorine ions, which led to corrosion of the tank walls, and the iron oxide from the corrosion in turn reacted exothermically with the methyl isocyanate. The increase in heat and pressure was rapid but unnoticed because the pressure gauge on the tank had been inoperable for four months and the operators in the control room monitoring a remote temperature gauge, were accustomed to higher-than-specified heat levels ($25°C$. rather then the $0°C$. in the operating instructions) due to the continual presence of the chloroform and some water vapor in the tank. The refrigeration unit built to cool the storage tank had been disconnected six months previously. The "scrubber," a safety device to neutralize the methyl isocyanate with caustic soda, had been under repair since June. An operator, alarmed by the suddenly increasing temperature, attempted to cool the tank by spraying it with water, but by then the reaction was unstoppable, at a probable $200°C$. The rupture disc (a steel plate in the line, to prevent accidental operation of the safety valve) broke, the safety valve opened (just before, it is assumed, the tank would have burst), and over half the 45 tons of methyl isocyanate in storage were discharged into the air.

Following the accident, Union Carbide officials in the United States denied strongly that their firm was responsible for the tragedy. They made the following three statements in support of that position:

1. *Limited authority.*   The Bhopal plant was 50.9% owned by the American firm, but the parent corporation had been able to exercise very little control. All managerial and technical personnel were citizens of India at the insistence of the Indian government. No Americans were permanently employed at the plant. Safety warnings from visiting American inspectors about the Sevin manufacturing process had been ignored.

2. *Limited safety.*   Five automatic safety devices that had originally been installed as part of the Sevin manufacturing process had, by the time of the accident, been either replaced by manual safety methods to increase employment, shut down for repairs, or disconnected as part of a cost reduction program. The automatic temperature and pressure warning signals had been removed soon after construction. The repairs on the automatic scrubber unit had extended over six months. The refrigeration unit had never been used to cool the tank and had been inoperable for over a year.

3. *Limited return.*   The Bhopal plant had been built in partnership with the Indian government to increase employment in that country. Union Carbide would have preferred to make Sevin in the United States and ship it to India for distribution and sale, because the insecticide could be made less expensively in the United States due to substantial economies of scale in the manufacturing process and much greater ease of supervision.

Warren Anderson, chairman of Union Carbide, stated that while he did not believe that the American company was legally liable for the tragedy due to the three points above, it was still "morally" responsible, and he suggested that the firm should pay prompt financial compensation to those killed and injured in the accident.

Class Assignment.   Assume that the question of legal liability for the accident at Bhopal will never be settled, due to differences in the law between the two countries and the difficulties of establishing both jurisdiction and blame. Assume, however, that the American company feels morally responsible for the tragedy, as admitted by the chairman, because it was the majority owner and yet did not firmly insist that the unsafe process be shut down. What factors would you consider in deciding upon "just" financial compensation for the victims?

CASE 2–3

U.S. Chemical Company

(disguised name)

Assume that you are product manager for a line of insecticides and pesticides produced by a large U.S. chemical company. Your responsibility is for both domestic and foreign sales, through foreign sales have been declining recently due to global competition. The chemical industry is exceedingly competitive, with large diversified firms operating in all of the economically advanced countries, while many basic chemicals are also now being produced in the developing nations as well. Assume that you have been able to meet the sales goals established for your product line, despite this competition, but only through offering substantial price concessions to major customers so that you now find yourself falling behind on your targeted return on assets. Return on assets employed—or ROA as it is more frequently termed—is a measure of financial performance; it is computed by dividing the pretax profits for a given product line by the total current and fixed assets employed by that product line.

You have an unusual opportunity to increase both your sales and profit figures by selling a pesticide known as Dicldrin to a group of foreign customers. Dieldrin is very toxic. It has been banned for use in the United States, Western Europe, and Japan. Chemical companies in Western Europe and Japan are forbidden to export the product, but that prohibition has never been adopted by the U.S. government. It happens that your company originally developed Dieldrin to control insects that infested cotton grown in the southeastern United States. The company has not produced it since 1978 when it was banned due to the observed build-up of toxic residues in birds and game animals and to the reported cases of illness among farm workers and their families. The company, however, could easily and inexpensively convert one of their existing processes to manufacture the chemical, and the expertise to supervise that process is still available within the firm.

You have received a request to produce and sell a large amount of Dieldrin from a regional agricultural authority representing many of the countries in North and East Africa. This is an area that has been plagued for centuries by swarms of locusts which are winged insects about 2-1/2″ to 3″ long. Locusts are very destructive. A single swarm will contain millions of insects, cover 5 to 10 square miles, and eat hundreds of tons of vegetation per day. They will strip crop land and trees bare, and then move on to a new area, in a cycle that lasts for two to three months. Before dying the female lays eggs in the soil and sand where they hatch into grubs. The unusual aspect of locusts is that the grubs do not necessarily mature into the winged or adult form the next year. A few do mature each year but the vast majority, depending upon the species, will wait three to seven years before they go into the cocoon state from which they emerge as a new swarm on almost exactly the same day during the spring and early summer. The spring and early summer is the most critical time for agriculture in the region because crops are grown on water stored in the soil from winter rains, and crops that are destroyed by the locust swarms cannot be replanted.

The destruction, however, is not complete throughout the region or even a single country because the locust swarms are scattered, and the damage occurs in a very patchwork fashion. Further, locusts are a known hazard and the country people keep stores of wheat in masonry silos, protected from those insects, for their own use. The locusts contribute to the poverty of the region, but they do not cause starvation or even mass malnutrition unless larger than normal swarms are accompanied by drought and/or political instability and war.

Perhaps 20% to 30% of the total crop is destroyed in a bad year, but the persons primarily affected are the landowners who suffer financial losses and the poor in the cities who are subject to price increases for wheat, their basic food source. The landowners in the region tend to be members of the governing class, while the poor in the cities are an unstabilizing political force, and consequently governments within the region tend to be active in measures to control the population of locusts.

Swarms of flying locusts are often sprayed with insecticides similar to DDT, which is another group of chemicals now banned for use in the United States, Europe, and Japan, but the technology for making DDT is widely known and the product has frequently been manufactured in the developing world. The problem is that quality control was occasionally neglected, low strength insecticides were evidently produced, and the locusts have gradually become immune to that form of control.

Dieldrin works on an entirely different basis. It kills locusts, and other insects which go through the grub stage, in the soil. It is very effective when used in proper strength, and there was never evidence—while it was legal to use in the United States—that the grubs could develop a tolerance and become immune.

The problem with Dieldrin is that it is a water soluble chemical, and does build up in the food chain. The precise effects of it, however, are not known. In the early 1970s, following the publication of Rachel Carson's landmark book *Silent Spring* which catalogued the decline of birds and other wild animals as a result of the widespread use of pesticides, Dieldrin was banned. New pesticides were developed, proven to be reasonably safe, and then approved for use in the United States. Western Europe and

Japan followed this lead during the late 1970s and early 1980s. No one fully investigated the older pesticides beyond the early studies which unquestionably did show harm to humans a well as wildlife.

The early studies—which, once again, are the only ones available—show that Dieldrin does build up in the liver, and can cause illnesses associated with the liver, particularly among young children. It is not clear, however, exactly how severe those illnesses are, nor the percentage that may lead to permanent damage or even death. One study showed that, in a rural county in the South where cotton was a major crop and Dieldrin had been extensively used, liver related illnesses increased about 4.8% in comparison to a generally similar "control" county where cotton was not grown. It should be recognized, however, that medical care was not widely extended to many farm families in the South at this time. And that as a consequence all of the incidents of liver related illnesses may not have been found in those counties. It should also be recognized that the original ban by the government was not arbitrary or autocratic; numerous accounts of illness and death among farm workers following the application of Dieldrin were reported in the newspapers.

You, as product line manager for insecticides at the United States Chemical Company, do not have time to institute more definitive studies even if a suitable location could be found. The agricultural authority, which represents all of the countries of North and East Africa, wants a supply of Dieldrin now. They have tried other insecticides, and none were more than partially effective. And, they expect a year with a particularly strong infestation of locusts.

The agricultural authority wishes to purchase $25 million worth of Dieldrin for prompt delivery. As your company is one of the few in the world with the technical capability and legal authority to make and sell the product to them, price competition will not be a factor and you can make your normal margin on the product. You have checked with the corporate attorney to make certain that you do have the legal authority to ship Dieldrin abroad; that person replied that he thought that such authority would be upheld in the courts, but that the ruling would be challenged if any environmental groups heard of the shipment.

You also made an appointment to discuss the possibility of this sale with the Senior Vice President for Agricultural Chemicals, who is the person to whom you report. He told you that, given the divisionalized "profit center" structure in which the company was organized, he did not feel that he should tell you what to do in this instance. "You're responsible for your own product line," he concluded as he walked with you to the door of his office, "I'm certain that you'll make the right decision."

Class Assignment.   What is the right decision? What would you do, faced with this situation? Please be ready to explain the reasons behind your response.

CHAPTER 3

Managerial Ethics
and the Rule of Law

In this chapter, we will look at the law as a possible basis for managerial decision when you are confronted with an ethical dilemma. The law is a set of rules, established by society, to govern behavior within that society. Why not, then, fall back upon those rules when faced with a conflict between the economic performance of an organization and the social performance of that organization? Why not let the law decide, particularly in a democratic society where the argument can easily be made that the rules within the law represent the collective moral judgments made by members of the society? Why not follow these collective moral judgments, instead of trying to establish our individual moral opinions?

There are numerous examples of laws that do reflect collective moral judgments. Almost everybody within the United States would agree that unprovoked assault is wrong; we have laws against assault. Almost everybody would agree that toxic chemical discharges are wrong; we have laws against pollution. Almost all of us would agree that charitable giving is right; we have no laws against charitable giving. Instead we have laws—provisions within the tax code—that encourage gifts of money, food, and clothing to the poor, and to organizations that work to assist the poor. The question of this chapter is whether we can use this set of rules—often complex, occasionally obsolete, and continually changing—to form "right" and "proper" and "fair" decisions when faced with a choice between our economic gains and our social obligations.

Let me give an illustration of the use of law to justify a decision in an ethical dilemma. The example is a situation that bankers face nearly every day: that between investing in a new, small company that will provide the local community with more job opportunities and higher tax payments to support schools and other needed social services, or loaning the same funds to an established, larger company operating in a distant city. The risk is obviously greater for the first investment, but banks are forbidden by law from charging usurious (too high, or excessive) interest rates to compensate for the risk.

How would you decide in that instance? It is possible, of course, to fall back upon the market and say that the law prohibiting usurious interest rates should be repealed, so that all companies would pay the true costs of their borrowings. Capital is one of the factors of production, along with labor and materials, and the microeconomic argument is that companies should pay prices determined by the factor markets. In this instance, the argument would be that the small, local company should pay the interest rate demanded by a free, efficient, and effective capital market. If the small local company were unable to pay this risk-adjusted rate, then the money should be invested elsewhere, at the next highest risk-adjusted rate that could be paid, in order to maximize the production of needed goods and services at minimal costs in the use of resources. As was seen in Chapter 2, there are both practical and theoretical problems with this view. The three practical problems are rather basic:

1. The exclusion of segments of society. The poor, because they lack ownership of any of the factors of production beyond their own unskilled labor, are often unable to participate in either the output product or the input factor markets.

2. The presence of injurious practices. Process pollutants, workplace hazards, and product dangers are not really issues in this bank loan example, but racial and sexual discrimination could affect the decision to make or not make the loan.

3. The absence of competitive markets. The input factor market for capital may not be fully price competitive because of the oligopolistic practices among the large financial institutions serving that market.

The microeconomic response to these three pragmatic problems is that society should add a political process to allocate some resources and require some actions, outside of the market process. This proposal, as was also seen in the last chapter, immediately encounters the objection that it requires individuals to be generously attentive to all other people in political decisions and selfishly attentive only to themselves in economic activities, and never confuse the two roles. This, it was concluded in that chapter, requires an exceedingly complex and unlikely view of the nature of human beings.

LAW AS A GUIDE TO MORAL CHOICE

We cannot rely upon the market as a guide for managerial decisions and actions when faced with an ethical dilemma, but how about the law? The legal argument is very different. The legal argument is that society has established a set of rules, and that these rules reflect the collective choices of members of society regarding any decisions and actions that affect the welfare of society. This argument can be applied to the particular instance of a bank officer forced to make up his or her mind between a high-risk loan to a small, local company with the return—the interest rate—limited by laws against usury, and an equivalent loan to a large, distant corporation at much lower risk but an equal return. The return on the loan to the large, distant corporation may even be higher than the return on the loan to the small, local firm if the lower administrative costs of loaning to large, well-financed corporations are included in the calculation. It can be said in this case that society has determined that usurious interest charges are more harmful than limited local support for new ventures, and that consequently the loan should be given to the larger, distant firm.

Should we object to this decision? Suppose we believe that it is necessary, for the good of our society, that the formation of small, entrepreneurial companies be encouraged. It is often said that if we don't like a given action by a corporation, we should attempt to pass a law either prohibiting that action or encouraging an alternative action, and if we cannot get that law approved through our democratic processes, then we should accept the situation as it exists. That is, we should rely upon the law in our decisions, and agree that if a given act is legal it is "right" and if it is illegal it is "wrong," with the understanding that these determinations of right and wrong can be changed to reflect the majority views of the population. In the example just given, of a bank refusing to advance funds to a high-risk company in the local community and instead providing capital to a lower-risk corporation in a distant city, it would be fairly easy to design corrective legislation. Each bank within the state, or within the nation, could be required to invest a certain percentage of its funds within the communities from which it drew those funds from depositors. This is an aside, of course, but that was essentially the result of the prior laws in most states that prohibited branch banking; local banks were forced to invest within their communities because they had few customer contacts outside of those communities. Deregulation of banks, which ended such territorial restrictions, has also stopped the local service orientation of many financial institutions.

It would also be fairly easy to design a law that would encourage investments in higher-risk, smaller companies. It would be possible, for example, to reduce the risk by providing a governmental guarantee for a given percentage of the loan. This, in effect, was the result of the loan guarantee program of the Small Business Administration—a division of the federal government in the Department of Commerce. Through this program, the government would repurchase 90 percent of the unpaid balance of approved loans in the event of borrower default. Another approach would be to provide a subsidy to the bank or other financial institution to supplement the limited interest rates that may be charged to high-risk companies. That was the effect of the Area Development and Business Investment programs, also from the Small Business Administration, that provided funds at below-market rates to financial institutions for reinvestment in smaller, local firms.

AN EXAMPLE OF MORAL CHOICE

Now, let us return to the banker in the example that was used in the introduction to this chapter. He or she is faced with the decision whether or not to invest in a high-risk local company that will provide employment opportunities and other benefits within the community. Let us agree that this is an ethical dilemma, though in a somewhat mild form, for the choice is between the economic performance of the bank, as measured by potential profits, and the social performance of the same bank, stated in terms of obligations to members of the community. I have suggested that this is a somewhat "mild" ethical dilemma, for no one is going to be hurt very badly by the banker's decision. There will be some employment opportunities lost, and some tax payments not made, but no one will suffer physical harm, as in the unsafe discharge of toxic wastes, or endure emotional stress, as from unfair firing brought about by age, sex, or race discrimination. So, let us strengthen the dilemma. Let us assume that the local community is in an area of high unemployment, that new jobs are badly needed, and that the proposed company is in a labor-intensive, high-growth industry and might eventually create many new jobs. Let us assume that the alternative investment, the large corporation in a distant city, is in a capital-intensive industry and that it would create few new jobs. Let us go even further and assume that the product of the proposed local company is a needed health-care item that would reduce the pain and suffering of elderly patients in hospitals throughout the country, while the product of the alternative investment possibility is a line of high-calorie packaged "junk" foods with low nutritional value. Last, let us not assume but accept the fact that the funds available through the Small Business Administration have been sharply curtailed in recent years and that no governmental guarantee or interest subsidy is available to support the loan to the smaller company. Now we have the classic ethical dilemma: the choice between economic performance and social performance, complicated by extended consequences, uncertain outcomes, and career implications.

How would you decide if faced with this choice? If the banker replies to the founders of the new small company that he or she would very much like to help but that the law prevents an adequate return to compensate for the risk, that no federal guarantees or interest subsidies are available, and that bank officers are required by the legal system to minimize risks for their depositors, can the banker truly be said to be wrong? Of course, the usual response of most bankers to socially desirable but financially shaky loans is not to explain the reasoning that led to the loan rejection. Instead, they merely suggest that the potential borrowers should seek funds elsewhere—where they doubtless will receive exactly the same response.

The question of this chapter is not whether banks should make socially desirable but economically unfeasible loans. Obviously, if the loan cannot be repaid, no bank can make a series of those loans and remain in business. But that is not the issue here. The question is how to make the decision—what factors to consider and what standards to use—in attempting to arrive at a balance between economic performance and social performance. There does have to be a balance. A bank can't make a series of economically feasible but socially undesirable loans either and expect to have the society continue to exist in a form that will enable the bank to prosper. There has to be a limit on both sides. There has to be a balance, and the question is how to achieve that balance.

LAW AS COMBINED MORAL JUDGMENTS

In the last chapter, we looked at the argument that you could achieve the balance between economic and social performance by considering only financial factors and using only economic standards. According to this argument market forces lead inevitably towards maximum social benefits at minimum social costs (Pareto Optimality), and those benefits can then be distributed equitably by a political process. We found that argument wanting. In this chapter we will look at the argument that you should consider both financial and social factors but use legal standards—the requirements of the law—in making ethical or "balanced" choices.

Numerous attorneys and business executives believe that you can base ethical decisions and actions on the requirements of the law. These people would say that if a law is wrong, it should be changed, but that until it is changed it provides a meaningful guide for action. It provides this guide for action, they would add, because each law within a democratic society represents a combined moral judgment by members of our society on a given issue or problem. They will concede that you and I might not agree personally with that judgment on a particular issue, but they would claim that if managers follow the law on that issue, those managers cannot truly be said to be wrong in any ethical sense, since they are following the moral standards of a majority of their peers.

Advocates of the rule of law—a phrase that means the primacy of legal standards in any given social or economic choice—will normally admit that the combined moral judgments represented by the law form a minimal set of standards: the basic rules for living together within a society without infringing on the rights of others. "If you want to go beyond the basic rules of the law in your own decisions and actions," they might say, "we certainly have no objection." "But," they would add, "you cannot require us to go beyond the law, for then you are forcing us to adhere to your moral standards, not those of a majority of the population. We live in a democracy, so, if you don't like something that we are doing, gather together a majority of the voters and pass a law restricting those actions, and we will obey that law. Until then, however, our moral standards are fully as valid as your own, and ours have the support of the majority of the population, so please do not lecture us on your views of what is right or wrong, proper and improper, fair and unfair.

How do we respond to those statements? And if it is not possible to respond logically and convincingly, are we forced to accept the rule of law as determinant in most moral dilemmas? I think that it is necessary first to define the law, so that all of us will recognize that we are discussing the same set of concepts, and then to examine the process—or processes—involved in formulating the law. This examination will be generally the same as in Chapter 2, Managerial Ethics and Microeconomic Theory, in which we looked at the role of market forces as determinants for managerial decisions in ethical dilemmas. However, legal/social/political theory is much less complete than microeconomic theory and there are numerous alternative hypotheses that will have to be considered briefly. First, however, let us define the law and expand on what is meant by the *rule of law*.

DEFINITION OF THE LAW

The law can be defined as a consistent set of universal rules that are widely published, generally accepted, and usually enforced. These rules describe the ways in which people are required to act in their relationships with others within a society. They are requirements to act in a given way, not just expectations or suggestions or petitions to act in that way. There is an aura of insistency about the law; it defines what you *must* do.

These requirements to act, or more generally requirements not to act in a given way—most laws are negative commandments, telling us what we should not do in given situations—have a set of characteristics that were mentioned briefly above. The law was defined as a consistent, universal, published, accepted, and enforced set of rules. Let us look at each of these characteristics in greater detail:

Consistent

The requirements to act or not to act have to be consistent to be considered part of the law. That is, if two requirements contradict each other, both cannot be termed a law, because obviously people cannot obey both.

Universal

The requirements to act or not to act also have to be universal, or applicable to everyone with similar characteristics facing the same set of circumstances, to be considered part of the law. People tend not to obey rules that they believe are applied only to themselves and not to others.

Published

The requirements to act or not to act have to be published, in written form, so that they are accessible to everyone within the society, to be considered part of the law. Everyone may not have the time to read or be able to understand the rules, which tend to be complex due to the need to precisely define what constitute similar characteristics and the same set of circumstances. However, trained professionals—attorneys—are available to interpret and explain the law, so that ignorance of the published rules is not considered to be a valid excuse.

Accepted

The requirements to act or not to act in a given way have to be generally obeyed. If most members of the society do not voluntarily obey the law, too great a burden will be placed on the last provision, that of enforcement.

Enforced

The requirements to act or not to act in a given way have to be enforced. Members of society have to understand that they will be compelled to obey the law if they do not choose to do so voluntarily. People have to recognize that if they disobey the law, and if that disobedience is noted and can be proven, they will suffer some loss of convenience, time, money, freedom, or life. There is an aura of insistency about the law; there is also, or should be, an aura of inevitability; it defines what will happen if you don't follow the rules.

This set of rules that are consistent, universal, published, accepted, and enforced—which we call *law*—is supported by a framework of highly specialized social institutions. There are legislatures and councils to form the law; attorneys and paralegal personnel to explain the law; courts and agencies to interpret the law; sheriffs and police to enforce the law. These social institutions often change people's perception of the law because the institutions are obviously not perfect. The adversary relationships within a trial court often seem to ignore the provisions of consistency and universality and to focus on winning rather than justice. The enforcement actions of the police also often seem to be arbitrary and to concentrate on keeping the peace rather than maintaining equity. Let us admit that enforcing the law is a difficult and occasionally dangerous task. Let us also admit that interpreting the law, in court cases, often involves the award of large amounts of money, and that the potential gain or loss of these funds—with attorneys on each side being paid a substantial percentage of that loss or gain—has distorted the concept of the law as a set of published and accepted regulations. But we are looking at the law as an ideal concept of consistent and universal rules to guide managerial decisions, not as a flawed reality.

RELATIONSHIPS BETWEEN THE LAW AND MORAL STANDARDS

If the law is viewed in ideal terms as a set of universal and consistent rules to govern human conduct within society, the question is whether we can accept these rules—flawed though they may be by pragmatic problems in interpretation and enforcement—as representing the collective moral judgment of members of our society. If we can, then we have the standards to guide managerial decisions and actions even though these standards may be at a minimal level. If we cannot accept the set of rules as representing the collective moral judgment of our society, then we will have to look elsewhere for our standards. In considering the possible relationship between moral judgments and legal requirements, there would seem to be three conclusions that can be reached fairly quickly:

1. The requirements of the law overlap to a considerable extent but do not duplicate the probable moral standards of society. Clearly, a person who violates the federal law against bank robbery also violates the moral standard against theft. And it is easy to show that the laws governing sexual conduct, narcotics usage, product liability, and contract adherence are similar to the moral beliefs that probably are held by a majority of people in our society. I think that we can agree that in a democratic society, the legal requirements do reflect many of the basic values of the citizens, and that there is an area of overlap between the law and morality (see Exhibit 3–1).

But the area of overlap is not complete. There are some laws that are morally inert, with no ethical content whatever. The requirement that we drive on the right-hand side of the road, for example, is neither inherently right nor inherently wrong; it is just essential that we all agree on which side we are going to drive. There are also some laws that are morally repugnant. Until the early 1960s, some areas of the United States legally required racial discrimination (segregated education, housing, and travel accommodations), and slavery was legally condoned just 100 years earlier. Finally, there are some moral standards that have no legal standing whatever. We all object to lying, but truthfulness is not required by law except in a court, under oath, and in a few other specific instances such as employment contracts and property sales.

EXHIBIT 3–1

Overlap between Moral Standards and Legal Requirements

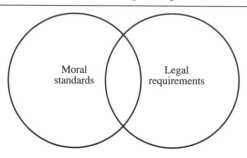

People who believe in the rule of law and accept legal regulations as the best means of governing human conduct within society would respond by saying that it is not at all clear that racial segregation was deplored by a majority of the population prior to 1962, or even that slavery was considered unconscionable before 1862. In a much lighter vein, concerning lying, they might even claim that most people have become accustomed to, and perhaps are amused by, a reasonable lack of truthfulness in advertising messages and political discourse. Moral standards, they would say, are difficult to determine, and we must be careful not to infer that our standards represent those held by a majority of the population.

2. The requirements of the law tend to be negative, while the standards of morality more often are positive. In the law, we are forbidden to assault, rob, or defame each other, but we are not required to help people, even in extreme situations. There is no law, for example, that we must go to the aid of a drowning child. Here, we do have a situation where the moral standards of the majority can be inferred, for doubtless 99.9 percent of the adult population within the United States would go to the aid of a drowning child, to the limit of their ability. People who support the rule of law, however, would say that this instance does not indicate a lack of relationship between moral standards and legal requirements; it only indicates the difficulty of translating one into the other when a positive—compassionate or charitable—act is needed. How, they would question, can you define in consistent and universal terms what is meant by assistance, the characteristics of the person who is to provide that assistance, and the circumstances under which it will be required? This, they would conclude, is just another illustration that the law represents the minimum set of standards to govern behavior in society and that actions beyond that minimum have to come from individual initiative, not legal force.

3. The requirements of the law tend to lag behind the apparent moral standards of society. Slavery, of course, is the most odious example, but sexual and racial discrimination, environmental pollution, and foreign bribery can all be cited as moral problems that were belatedly addressed by legislation. Advocates of the rule of law would say, however, that the evidence of a delay between apparent moral consensus and enacted legal sanctions does not necessarily indicate a lack of relationship between legal requirements and moral standards. It only serves to confirm that relationship, they would claim, for laws controlling discrimination, pollution, and bribery were eventually passed.

None of these arguments—that legal requirements overlap but do not duplicate moral standards, or that the legal requirements appear in different forms (negative rather than positive) and at different times (sequential rather than concurrent)—seems truly decisive. None really helps to determine whether the law really does represent a collective moral judgment by members of a democratic society and consequently can serve to guide managerial decisions and actions. We can easily say that the law does not represent our moral judgment in a given situation, but how can we say that the law in that instance does not represent the moral judgment of a majority of our peers? For that, I think, we have to follow through the process by which our society has developed the law as a universal and consistent set of rules to govern human conduct.

FORMATION OF THE LAW: INDIVIDUAL PROCESSES

Law is obviously a dynamic entity, for the rules change over time. Think of the changes that have occurred in the laws governing employment, for example, or pollution. This is essentially the same point that was made previously, that there seems to be a time lag between changes in moral standards and changes in legal requirements, but actions that were considered to be legal twenty years ago—such as racial and sexual discrimination in hiring, or the discharge of chemical wastes into lakes and streams—are now clearly illegal. The question is whether these changes in the law came from changes in the moral standards of a majority of our population through a social and political process, and consequently whether the law does represent the collective moral standards of our society. The social and political process by which the changing moral standards of individual human beings are alleged to become institutionalized into the formal legal framework of society is lengthy and complex, but a simplified version can be shown in graphic form (see Exhibit 3–2).

Each individual within society has a set of norms, beliefs, and values that together form his or her moral standards. Norms, of course, are criteria of behavior. They are the ways an individual expects all people to act, when faced with a given situation. Foreign students from certain Asiatic countries, for example, bow slightly when addressing a university professor; the bow is their norm or expectation of behavior given that situation. University faculty members within the United States are generally somewhat annoyed when this occurs; their norm or expectation of behavior in that situation is considerably less formal and

EXHIBIT 3–2
Process by which Individual Norms, Beliefs, and Values Are Institutionalized into Law

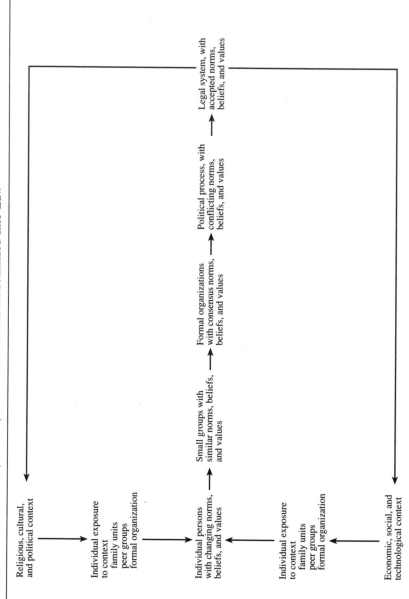

more egalitarian. The depth of the bow and the degree of annoyance both decline over time as the expectations of behavior on both sides are modified through learning.

Another example of a norm of behavior is considerably less facetious and more relevant to the discussion of moral standards and the law. Most people expect that others, when they meet them, should not cause them injury. Norms are expectations of the ways people ideally should act, not anticipations of the ways people really will act. A person who holds a norm against assault and robbery—as most of us do—will not ordinarily walk down a dark street in the warehouse district of a big city at three in the morning; he or she feels that people should not assault and rob each other, not that they will not do so.

Norms are expectations of proper behavior, not requirements for that behavior. This is the major difference between a norm and a law; the norm is not published, may not be obeyed, and cannot be enforced—except by the sanctions of a small group whose members hold similar norms and use such penalties as disapproval or exclusion. Norms also are often neither consistent nor universal. The person who actually commits a crime in the warehouse district at three in the morning, feeling it permissible to assault and rob someone else given the situation and need, doubtless would feel outraged if assaulted and robbed in the same place and at the same time the next night. Norms are just the way we feel about behavior; often they are neither logically consistent nor universally applied because we have never thought through the reasons we hold them.

Beliefs are criteria of thought; they are the ways an individual expects people to think about given concepts. I believe in participatory democracy, for example, and I expect others to recognize the worth of that concept and accept it as a form of government. I believe in environmental preservation also, and I expect other people to recognize the importance of that idea and accept it as a goal worth working towards.

Beliefs are different from norms in that they involve no action—no overt behavior towards others—just an abstract way of thinking that tends to support an individual's norms. Asiatic students who bow to American professors believe, it is alleged, in a hierarchical society, with definite gradations between older faculty and younger students. People who hold the norm that others should not assault and rob them, even on darkened streets and in deserted neighborhoods, generally believe in the worth of human beings and the preservation of personal property. In one last example, the norm that a company should not bury toxic wastes in leaking 55-gallon drums is associated with beliefs about the benefits of a clean environment and the adverse effects of chemical pollution upon individual health.

Values, the last third of this pattern of personal criteria that together form the moral standards of an individual, are the rankings or priorities that a person establishes for his or her norms and beliefs. Most people do not consider that all their norms and beliefs are equal in importance; generally there are some that seem much more important than others. The important norms and beliefs are the ones that a person "values," or holds in high esteem.

Values often are controversial. Why? Because a norm or belief that one person holds in high esteem can conflict with a different norm or belief that another person holds in equally high esteem. Generally there will be little accommodation or compromise, because each person attaches great importance to his or her criteria of behavior—ways in which people ought to act—and to his or her criteria of belief—ways in which people ought to think. We live in a pluralistic society, with numerous cultural traditions, and in a secular nation, with no accepted or endorsed religious heritage; consequently we have to live with the fact that norms, beliefs, and values will differ among individuals. These differences can and do lead to conflicts.

The norms, beliefs, and values of an individual together form that person's moral standards. Moral standards are our means of judging whether an act that affects others is "right" or "wrong," and they are based upon our personal valuation or ranking of our norms—criteria of behavior— and of our beliefs—criteria of thought. For example, I value highly my norm of nonaggressive behavior between members of our society; if I come out of my house on a summer morning and you hit me on the head and steal my wallet, I am going to consider what you have done to be "wrong." I value less highly my belief in the benefits of a clean environment; if I come out of my house the next day and find you pouring used motor oil down the drain in the street, I am going to think of you as a fairly despicable person, for I would consider that act to be "wrong" also, but less wrong than your previous assault and robbery.

Moral standards—the criteria we use for judging whether an act that impacts others is right or wrong—for now can be considered to be subjective, that is, the result of each individual's emotional preferences among a range of possible norms and beliefs. In the next chapter, Managerial Ethics and Normative Philosophy, we will consider the possibility that moral standards might be seen as objective, or rationally derived from a single fundamental norm or absolute belief. An example of a fundamental norm would be, Always act to generate the greatest good for the greatest number. An example of an absolute belief would be, Justice is the basic essential for a cooperative society. A fundamental norm or absolute belief, if accepted by an individual, would objectively determine that person's complete set of moral standards, because all of his or her other norms and beliefs could be logically derived, in an orderly ranking or value system, from that single principle or truth. A fundamental norm or absolute belief, if accepted by all members of society, would lead to consistent moral standards throughout society, for the same reason. For the present discussion, however, it is necessary to admit that our society lacks such a single principle or truth. This is not to say that we should not have an accepted basis for consistent moral standards; it is just to say that we presently do not have that accepted basis.

FORMATION OF THE LAW: GROUP PROCESSES

Each individual has a set of norms, beliefs, and values that subjectively determine his or her moral standards. These moral standards are at least partially unique to each person, as they are based upon emotional selection rather than rational determination. Most adult members of society recognize their individual set of standards, but few of us have examined or considered these standards beyond a general understanding of mutual reciprocity and social continuance. "I should not assault and rob others because then they would feel free to assault and rob me" and "I should not assault and rob others because no society can continue to exist if assault and robbery are constant occurrences" are both moral statements, though based upon slightly different sets of norms, beliefs, and values. "I should not assault and rob others because I might get caught and put in jail" is more a legal concern than a moral standard, and it is based upon a very different set of norms, beliefs, and values.

Each individual develops his or her set of norms, beliefs, and values through exposure to a cultural/religious/political context and a social/economic/technological context. Context means the general background or surrounding environment of a situation; the literal derivation of the word is from the Latin "woven together," and that almost exactly conveys the meaning that is intended here. Each society has a background or environment that consists of interwoven threads from religious teachings, cultural traditions, political methods, social organizations, economic conditions, and technological developments. The interwoven nature of the context within which individual choices on norms, beliefs, and values are made ensures that all of these factors interact. Technological changes in communication bring political changes in governance, which cause economic changes in spending and taxation patterns, which eventually result in social changes in individual associations and cultural changes in personal lifestyle. The exact relationships between economic, technological, social, political, cultural, and religious factors are not known, nor can their combined influences upon an individual's norms, beliefs, and values be predicted with accuracy. But the relationships and influences can easily be observed. Think of the changing status of women, for example, which must have had some origin in the economic shift from heavy manufacturing and mining to knowledge-based and service industries, in the technological development of better birth-control methods, and in the social expansion of educational opportunities. Another illustration of a change in norms, beliefs, and values would be the widespread concern with preservation of the physical environment that developed during the 1960s, and was doubtless influenced by the economic prosperity and political activism of that period.

FORMATION OF THE LAW: SOCIAL PROCESSES

All individuals within a society do not have the same exposures to economic, technological, social, political, cultural, and religious factors. Such exposures come from individual positions, family units, peer groups, and formal organizations. For example, a steel worker who has been unemployed for a number of years due to the closing of a steel mill is directly exposed to the economic reality of international competition; children of the steel worker are indirectly but forcefully exposed through the family unit; associates of the steel worker are indirectly and more lightly exposed through peer groups such as neighborhood associations or social clubs and through formal organizations such as churches and banks. The norms, beliefs, and values of people throughout the industrialized cities that were heavily dependent upon steel, such as Buffalo, Pittsburgh, and Youngstown, have changed over the past 10 years, but to varying degrees, depending upon each individual's exposure to the underlying economic and technological factors.

The changing norms, beliefs, and values of individuals within society do, in a democratic society, have an apparent though delayed impact upon the law. This impact would appear to be the result of both social and political processes. The social process involves, basically, an accretion of power. People with similar norms, beliefs, and values tend to become associated in small groups; it is just natural to join others who have parallel views. These small groups generally are part of much larger organizations, such as business firms, labor unions, political parties, charitable agencies, religious institutions, and veterans' associations, and these larger organizations over time either achieve an acceptable compromise on norms, beliefs, and values, or split into smaller organizations that can achieve such a compromise. There are alternative theories on the means by which this compromise is formed: autocratic decision, bureaucratic adjustment, coalition bargaining, or collective choice. Doubtless all these methods are employed to different degrees in different organizations, but the outcome that can be observed is that many organizations do display a culture of shared norms, beliefs, and values that does gradually change over time.

FORMATION OF THE LAW: POLITICAL PROCESSES

The political process by which the norms, beliefs, and values held by organizations, groups, and individuals are institutionalized into law can be seen basically as a means of resolving conflict. Organizations, groups, and individuals obviously have different opinions on what should be done now (norms) and what should be accomplished in the future (beliefs), and these different views have to be reconciled into consistent and universal rules to be effective. Again, there are alternative theories on the ways by which this is done: presidential leadership, institutional compromise, congressional bargaining, and constituent pressure. The terms would differ at the federal, state, and local levels, but the process doubtless remains approximately the same. The leader, whether president, governor, or mayor, can speak of long-term objectives and attempt to gather support, but he or she has little direct influence on the lawmaking mechanism. Governmental departments and agencies and nongovernmental lobbying organizations provide the support with information, arguments, and campaign assistance but often must compromise their positions to work jointly and not cancel out each other's influence. Elected representatives are formally assigned responsibility for the formulation of laws in a representative system, but issues differ by section of the country, segment of the population and sector of the economy, and consequently there often seems to be bargaining to establish coalitions to pass most legislation. The public, of course, can express opinions on potential laws by voting for some administrators and all legislators, and indirectly through public surveys, letters, and the media.

The political process by which laws are enacted represents a complex series of interactions. Doubtless no one except a member of Congress or one of the state legislatures fully appreciates the extent and time demands of the formal hearings, office meetings, and committee reports, the constant interruptions and informal exchanges that occur in hallways, parking lots, and evening receptions, and the honest efforts that are made to summarize opinions from the electorate expressed in letters, telephone calls, and the media. All of these help to form the opinions of the legislators. It is easy to be cynical when thinking of the political process, particularly when the high cost of election campaigns is considered and the need to raise money to finance those campaigns is included, but it is difficult to invent a better process than representative democracy.

CONCLUSIONS ON THE RULE OF LAW AS THE BASIS FOR MORAL CHOICE

The question now is whether these social and political processes, lengthy and complex though they may be, truly do serve to combine the personal moral standards of a majority of our population, slowly and gradually, into universal legal requirements. That is, does the law actually represent the collective moral judgment of a majority of our population, or does it just consist of a set of official commands determined by unresponsive legislators? The view that the law does represent collective moral judgment is certainly appealing. However, there would seem to be problems in the transfer from individual moral standards to universal legal requirements at each of the stages in the social and political process.

1. The moral standards of members of society may be based upon a lack of information relative to issues of corporate conduct. Most people were apparently unaware of the payments of large foreign bribes until the revelations of the Lockheed case and the subsequent Securities and Exchange Commission study. Many people now may be unaware of the magnitude of the toxic waste-disposal problem, with 231 million metric tons being produced annually. It is difficult for personal moral standards to influence the law if relevant information is missing.

2. The moral standards of members of society may be diluted in the formation of small groups. People with similar norms, beliefs, and values tend to become associated in small groups, but these standards generally are not precisely similar among all members, and compromises have to be made. Further, many small groups act from motives other than morality; economic benefits and professional prestige often seem to be stressed. It is difficult for personal moral standards to influence the law if they are not conveyed accurately.

3. The moral standards of members of society may be misrepresented in the consensus of large organizations. Many organizations do share norms, beliefs, and values, but there is no evidence that each individual and each group within the organization has equal influence, or even equal weighted influence, in determining that consensus. This can be seen in the norms, beliefs, and values of many nonprofit organizations such as hospitals and universities; the standards of the professional personnel—the physicians and the faculty—often seem to predominate.

4. The moral standards of members of society may be misrepresented in the formulation of the laws. This is the same point that was made above in shaping the consensus of an organization, though on a larger scale. There is no guarantee that all organizations have equal influence, or even equal influence weighted by size, in determining the law. This can be seen in the provisions of much tax legislation; certain organizations always seem to be favored.

5. The legal requirements formed through the political process are often incomplete or imprecise and have to be supplemented by judicial court decisions or administrative agency actions. This can be seen in both product liability cases and equal employment reviews; the meaning and the application of the law have to be clarified outside of the legislative process. It is difficult for personal moral standards to influence the law if they are considered only indirectly—if at all—in two of the means of formulating that law.

What can we say in summary? We can observe that there obviously is an overlap between the moral standards and the legal requirements of our society—the federal law against bank robbery and the moral standard against stealing, for example. And we can see that some changes in the norms, beliefs, and values of individual members of society are eventually reflected by changes in the law—the Foreign Corrupt Practices Act and the Federal Air Pollution Control Act, for example. But we will have to admit that there is no direct relationship in all instances. The social and political processes by which the law is formulated are too complex and too cumbersome—and perhaps too subject to manipulation—for changes in people's norms, beliefs, and values to be directly translated into changes in that set of universal and consistent rules that we call law. Consequently, we cannot view this set of rules as representing the complete collective moral judgment of our society, and therefore we cannot rely totally on the rules when confronted by an ethical dilemma.

The law is a guide to managerial decisions and actions, but it is not enough. And certainly, the absence of a law is not enough to excuse some of those decisions and actions. We need something more. In the next chapter we will look at the fundamental norms and absolute values of normative philosophy as a possible means of providing that "something more."

CASE 3–1

When Is It Permissible to Break the Law?

The phrase "to break the law" doubtless is overly dramatic as a title for this series of short cases. Only two of the situations described below actually involve people acting in ways that are directly contrary to existing U.S. laws. The others involve situations where there seems to be a conflict between the applicable U.S. law and generally accepted practice within this country or abroad, or where the relevant U.S. laws have never been extended to cover the situation as described:

1. *Painting billboards in New York City.* It is, of course, illegal to deface private property and doubtless a claim could be made that it is especially illegal to deface advertising billboards because that act would interfere with the freedom of speech of the advertising firms. Despite that illegality, a group of church members from Harlem in New York City have begun whitewashing billboards advertising cigarettes, liquor and beer in the inner city. Armed with ladders, long-handled rollers, and buckets of white paint, they have simply painted over advertisements for the offending products. One of the leaders of the group has been quoted as saying, "We have to stop these efforts to market unhealthy products to neighborhoods already overcome by poverty, disease and despair."[1] In your opinion, is it right to break the law against defacing private property, given that the products being advertised do harm the health of the individuals who buy them?

2. *Reporting improper practices by an auditing client.* Federal law, AICPA rules, and generally accepted accounting standards all prohibit disclosing confidential information gained during the performance of an audit. In the event that accounting irregularities are discovered, it is expected that the auditing firm will either resign from the assignment or issue an adverse opinion. In the event that nonaccounting irregularities are discovered, such as lax safety practices, self-serving managerial decisions, or illegal political contributions, it has never been determined exactly what actions are required by the auditing firm, beyond the overriding prohibition against public disclosure. In your opinion, is it right to break this law against public disclosure of confidential information, given let us say that an auditing firm does discover evidence of very hazardous chemical wastes being buried close to a populated area and the company involved refuses to stop the practice?

3. *Approving indirect payments to foreign officials.* Many large U.S. manufacturers now operate abroad in sections of the world where cash payments to government officials in return for purchase contracts, import privileges or tax concessions may be illegal under local law, but are still either acknowledged or tolerated by local custom. U.S firms are legally forbidden to make these payments, under terms of the Foreign Corrupt Practices Act. European and Japanese companies are not similarly constrained, and it is said that their ability to follow local custom has enabled them to receive many of the contracts, privileges, and concessions that formerly went to the U.S. firms. It is also now said that many of the U.S. firms have adopted the practice of hiring local consultants who claim to be able to obtain the contracts, etc. "legitimately." The invoices from the local consultants, however, are generally 20% above the amounts of the requested bribes, which has led to the suspicion that the consultants are simply paying the bribes in lieu of the U.S. firms. In your opinion is it permissible to make these indirect payments?

4. *Rewarding company employees for "whistle-blowing" against their employer.* A very large manufacturer of aircraft bolts and fasteners on the West Coast recently paid an $18.0 million fine for the falsification of test results. Aircraft bolts and fasteners have to be exceedingly high quality: lightweight yet strong, and very resistant to corrosion and metal fatigue. The metallurgical tests that confirm these qualities are destructive in nature—that is, they destroy the part that is being tested—

and consequently they generally are not repeated by the purchasers of the fasteners, who instead rely upon a written certification of testing. The company admitted in this instance that many of the certified tests had never been performed. The prosecuting attorney admitted in return that no accidents had been traced to the untested fasteners, and that "most" of the company's bolts and fasteners still in inventory or now in use did meet "most" of the original specifications.

The two employees who had reported the test falsifications to the federal government, and who had provided secretly videotaped proof of those falsifications, received an award of 25% of the fine under the provisions of a 1988 federal law that was designed to encourage "whistle-blowing." An aircraft industry executive described his concerns verbally as follows: "No one is defending the practice of falsifying quality checks on critical aircraft components, but the federal government is paying two employees $2.25 million each for spying on their employer. The federal government is bribing the employees of private companies." In your opinion, is it right for the federal government to pay company employees very substantial amounts of money to report company wrong-doing, given that in the past (without the payments) many similar wrong-doings did go unreported?

Class Assignment. Decide which of these actions are "right" and which are "wrong." Follow your own opinion, but be prepared to support that opinion. Then, start thinking about how these situations developed. Do the senior executives at each of these firms (except for the first instance in which it is obvious that everyone knows of the situation, and for the last instance, in which it would be the senior officials in the government who must have approved) know what is happening? What, if anything, would you do if you were one of the senior executives (or officials) and did know of the situation?

Footnote

1. *New York Times,* April 10, 1989, p. 3.

CASE 3–2

Susan Shapiro

Susan Shapiro had an undergraduate degree in Chemistry from Smith College, a master's degree in Chemical Engineering from M.I.T., three years' service as a sergeant in the Israeli army, and an MBA from the

University of Michigan. The following is a nearly verbatim account of her experiences during the first month of employment with a large chemical company in New York.

We spent about three weeks in New York City, being told about the structure of the company and the uses of the products, and then they took us down to Baton Rouge to look at a chemical plant. You realize that most of the MBAs who go to work for a chemical company have very little knowledge of chemistry. There were 28 of us who started in the training program that year, and the others generally had undergraduate degrees in economics or marketing. I don't know what you learn by looking at a chemical plant, but they flew us down South, put us up at a Holiday Inn, and took us on a tour of their plant the next day.

As part of the tour, we were taken into a drying shed where an intermediate chemical product was being washed with benzine and then dried. The cake was dumped in a rotating screen and sprayed with benzine, which was then partially recovered by a vacuum box under the screen. However, the vacuum box technology is out-of-date now, and never did work very well. Much of the solvent evaporated within the shed, and the atmosphere was heavy with the fumes despite the "open air" type of construction.

Benzine is a known carcinogen; there is a direct, statistically valid correlation between benzine and leukemia and birth defects. The federal standard is 10 parts per million, and a lab director would get upset if you let the concentration get near 100 parts for more than a few minutes, but in the drying shed it was over 1,000. The air was humid with the vapor, and the eyes of the men who were working in the area were watering. I was glad to get out, and we were only in the drying shed about three minutes.

I told the foreman who was showing us around—he was a big, burly man with probably 30 years' experience—that the conditions in the shed were dangerous to the health of the men working there, but he told me, "Lady, don't worry about it. That is a sign-on job (a job to which newly hired employees are assigned until they build up their seniority so that they can transfer to more desirable work). We've all done it, and it hasn't hurt any of us."

That night, back at the motel, I went up to the director of personnel who was in charge of the training program and told him about the situation. He was more willing to listen than the foreman, but he said essentially the same thing. "Susan, you can't change the company in the first month. Wait awhile; understand the problems, but don't be a troublemaker right at the start."

The next morning everybody else flew back to New York City. I stayed in Baton Rouge and went to see the plant manager. I got to his office by 8:00, and explained to his secretary why I wanted to see him. He was already there, at work, and he came out to say that he was "up against it that morning" and had no time to meet with me. I said, "Fine, I'll wait."

I did wait, until after lunchtime. Then he came up to me and said he didn't want to keep tripping over me every time he went in and came out of his office, and if I would just go away for awhile, he would promise to see me between 4:30 and 5:00.

It was 5:15 when he invited me to "come in and explain what has you so hot and bothered." I told him. He said that he certainly knew what I was talking about, and that every year he put a capital request into the budget to fix the problem, but that it always came back rejected—"probably by some MBA staff type" were his words—because the project could not show an adequate return on investment, and because the present process was technically "open air" and therefore not contrary to OSHA regulations.

I started to explain that OSHA never seemed to know what it was doing—which is true, in my opinion. But he stopped me. He said that he was leaving to pick up his family because his daughter was playing in a Little League baseball game at 6:30, and then they would have supper at McDonald's. He said I could go along, if I didn't mind sitting next to his five year old son "who held the world's record for the number of consecutive times he has spilled his milk in a restaurant." He was a very decent man, working for a very indecent company. I told him I would go back to New York, and see what I could do. He did wish me "good luck," but he also asked me not to get him personally involved because he thought that "insisting upon funding for a project that won't meet targeted rates of return is a surefire way to be shown the door marked exit in large black letters."

Class Assignment. What would you do in this situation? Make a set of specific recommendations for Susan Shapiro.

CASE 3–3

Violence on Television

By the age of 18, the typical child has seen 13,000 killings and 100,000 other assorted acts of violence on television. These "assorted acts of violence" are not cartoon cats being hit on the head by cartoon mice; they include rapes, beatings, assaults, explosions, fires, street robberies, home entries, gang confrontations, car crashes, and police arrogance if not police brutality. In 1989 80% of all adult programs contained some violence, with an average of 9.5 violent events per hour. The adult programs containing violence originally are shown after 8:00 in the evening, when children's viewing is restricted to some extent, but the more popular—which often means the more violent—series generally are syndicated and eventually shown as reruns in the late afternoon, a period of high child exposure.

It is estimated that the average home has 1.8 television sets, and that the typical television set is turned on 52 hours per week. Everyone in the family, of course, does not watch during all of the 52 hours, and for much of the time no one is in the room or paying attention to the programs and advertisements. Children, however, do watch a lot of television. Children between the ages of two and five typically watch 28 hours per week. Children between the ages of six and eleven watch 23 hours per week. Children between the ages of twelve and seventeen watch 21 hours per week. This means that by age eighteen children will have spent 19,500 hours watching television, which contrasts with the 14,000 hours they will have spent attending school.

Much of this watching is unsupervised. More and more families are single parent households or households in which both parents work, so that in the afternoon no adult may be in the home to request that children change the channel. Those requests may not be common, even in the evening. A 1989 survey reported that 85% of all parents said that they gave their children no guidance in watching television either after school or during the evening.[1]

In summary, children are exposed to extensive violence on television, and that exposure is almost continual throughout the periods (late afternoon and early evening) they are most likely to be watching. The question, of course, is whether this continual exposure to extensive violence influences their own behavior. That is, does violence on television lead to violence in real life?

There is no question but that violence in real life is present within the United States. In 1989 on a national basis there was a murder every 24 minutes, a rape every 6 minutes, a robbery every 55 seconds, and an aggravated assault every 33 seconds. Moreover, it is believed that less than 50% of all nonlethal crimes are reported, so that the actual figures may far higher.

There is also no question but that violence has increased within the United States since the middle of the century, a period of time that correlates almost exactly with the increase in the popularity of television. The figures below show the increase in violent crimes against individuals since 1950, and are expressed as the numbers of crimes per 100,000 citizens in order to index out the influence of the increase in total population.[2]

	1950	1960	1970	1980	1990
Murders	5.1	9.0	16.0	23.0	23.4
Rapes	n.a.	17.0	38.0	83.0	102.6
Robberies	50.0	107.0	350.0	566.0	639.0
Assaults	73.0	152.0	335.0	673.0	1,093.0

The twelvefold increase in assaults is seen as the most telling statistic by those who believe that there is a direct relationship between violence on television and aggressiveness in real life. Assaults are physical confrontations that are not connected with the theft of money or property. Assaults are the result of disagreements over conduct that go beyond verbal abuse. They are ubiquitous. They occur in family homes, city streets, parking lots, suburban schools, college gyms, and softball diamonds. People disagree over who was first or who was right or who was responsible, and those disagreements seem to escalate into violence much more rapidly now than in the past.

It is easy to make the claim that the increases in murders, rapes and robberies are related to other changes within American society: the proo ence of drugs, the decay of neighborhoods, the repression of minorities, the lack of opportunities in housing, jobs and education. But, assaults are gratuitous violence. There is no sexual gratification. There is no monetary gain. There is just pain, humiliation, and defeat. Those are not related to the decline of neighborhoods; they are related to the decline in civility. (Statement of proponent of television reform)

The question, then, is whether the very substantial increase in the amount of violence shown on television has led to the very substantial increase in the number of personal assaults reported to police through a lessening of the degree of civility and the regard for others.

There are two levels on which this question whether violence on television is related to violence in real life can be answered. The first is the quantitative level: what do scientists have to say as the result of their empirical studies? The second is the qualitative level: what do law enforcement personnel, social workers, political figures, education experts, and industry executives have to say as a result of their personal experiences?

There have been literally thousands of empirical studies both in the United States and abroad. Parents have recorded the television viewing habits of younger children, and then social scientists have observed the interactions of those children to detect aggressive tendencies. "How would I respond to a given situation" questionnaires have been distributed to older children, before and after viewing television programs with graphically depicted violence. Playground situations have been observed in different countries with different television viewing patterns and different cultural imperatives.

What conclusions can be drawn from the full collection of studies? First, researchers have firmly established a positive correlation between the viewing of violent television and the aggressive behavior of children. Nearly everyone agrees on this and the proof seems virtually irrefutable. However, the correlation is weak, and—even further—correlation does not necessarily mean causation. It is still not clear whether: 1) viewing a lot of violent TV causes children to act aggressively; 2) acting aggressively causes children to watch a lot of violent TV; or 3) some third, unknown factor causes children to both watch violent TV and act aggressively.

For most nonacademics who are interested in the topic of violence on television it is probably fair to say that these inconclusive results have been disappointing. However, inconclusive and disappointing results may be a natural outcome of all social science research into important national problems. Too many variables may be involved. Many of those variables may be difficult to define and then measure. It is impossible to set up a control group (one that has either been isolated from or exposed to certain variables) because of the potential conflict with human rights.

People who support the status quo—the unrestricted showing of violence on television—start with the claim that violence is part of American life. Like it or not, they say, murders occur every 24 minutes within the United States, robberies every 55 seconds, and assaults every 33 seconds. It is legitimate to portray that violence on television, they claim, because otherwise the programs would just be sugarcoated fantasies, far from the reality of everyday life.

And, say people who support the status quo, violence is part of the world's literature. Murder mysteries are among the most popular of all books; should those novels be banned? Cowboy westerns are widely available; should they be removed from the shelves? Even classics such as Shakespeare's *MacBeth*, and children's stories such as *Little Red Riding Hood*, contain violence. *MacBeth* assassinates both Banquo and Duncan before being slain himself by MacDuff. *Little Red Riding Hood's* grandmother is eaten by the wolf, who then is hacked to death by the woodsman. Why is violence acceptable in *MacBeth* and *Little Red Riding Hood*, they ask, but not on *Murder She Wrote*?

People who oppose the portrayal of violence on television counter the claim that the programs simply reflect the violence of American life by saying that the violence currently shown on television is excessive in amount. The number of violent acts per hour, they claim, is well beyond anything experienced in real life. *Hard Ball*, which aired on NBC in the fall off 1989, averaged 47 violent acts per hour. That same year, *Tour of Duty* on CBS averaged 45 violent acts per hour, and *The Young Riders* on ABC averaged 40 acts per hour. Most people do not experience one-tenth of that violence within their entire lifetime, let alone the full amount within one hour. Police shows, some of which have topped over 50 violent acts per hour, are said to be even more unrealistic. The critics of violence on television explain that it is a fact that most police officers never fire their guns, except on the practice range, during their entire careers, and that most arrests are made without a struggle let alone a lengthy fight.

The critics also claim that the violence that is shown on television is excessive in its realism. They admit that violence is part of world literature, but explain that there is a vast difference between the verbal and the visual depiction of murders, beatings, and assaults. In *MacBeth*, for example, the killing of Duncan is not even verbally described by Shakespeare; instead the murder is encouraged by Lady MacBeth and later her husband reports, "T'is done." Television, the critics say, would graphically show the swordplay, with Duncan staggering slowly and bloodily towards his death. They make the same point with *Little Red Riding Hood*. It is one thing for a child to read (or have read to him/her) that "the woodsman swung his ax and killed the big, bad wolf;" it is another to portray that death with all the visual imagery of modern-day, full-color, high-resolution television.

Those who support the status quo also rely heavily on the research finding that the correlation between violence shown on TV and violence committed in real life is weak, and that the causation of one by the other cannot be proven. People on the other side counter with the fact that the correlation does exist, and that important social issues are difficult to investigate using empirical research methods:

> Unhappily, all of the major premises on which our society rests derive from the realm of intuition. Can anyone prove that the family is a desirable institution? That higher education promotes human welfare? That love is better than hate? That democracy is superior to dictatorship? None of these is provable. But this does not stop us from acting on our best judgment, knowing that all human judgment is fallible.[3]

Others have explained that policy makers and business managers usually have to make decisions based upon incomplete information, and that common sense often substitutes for scientific evidence:

> Methodological squabbles and the call for "more definitive research" have served as an excuse to buy time for producers. In my opinion, we do not need more research on the latest forms of violence to take action. As concerned citizens all of us need to raise the discourse to a moral level, a level in which we talk about the commonweal and what we want to teach our children.[4]

Still others who object to the violence currently shown on television say that network executives are being hypocritical when they claim that there is no proof that hours of viewing television violence have any major impact upon the behavior of children. These critics go on to say that there is no proof that hours of viewing television ads have any major impact upon the behavior of consumers. There is a weak correlation here, but no scientific evidence of causality, just as there is a weak correlation but no scientific evidence of causality in the case of violence on television and the behavior of children.

> You cannot prove that advertising a given headache pill or cold remedy leads to increased sales of those products. There is a correlation between the two, but you can't prove causality from advertising to sales. Network

executives are willing to accept one assumption of causal relationship, but eager to deny the other. That is pure hypocrisy. (Verbal statement of industry critic)

Lastly, many television and advertising executives say that it is up to the parents to supervise what their children can watch rather than attempting to censor what the networks can show. These executives add that a code presently exists which precludes gratuitous or excessive violence, and that "violence is only presented when there is a legitimate and thematic justification for its inclusion; that is when it is directly related to plot development and character delineation."[5]

Critics, of course, object to both proposals. They say that most parents work outside the home, and are consequently unable to supervise television watching habits as thoroughly as they would wish, and that industry self-regulation simply is not working or the number of violent acts that meet "legitimate and thematic justification for inclusion" would not be so high.

Throwing the full responsibility on the parents for determining what their children are exposed to is, in this day, naive and almost impossible. Parents need the help of the community with its various protective agencies and resources.[6]

I do not understand why network executives cannot adopt the simple rule that the amount of violence shown on television in one evening cannot exceed the amount of violence experienced by the typical viewer during one lifetime. But, that is not going to happen. As long as television people believe that violence sells, it's going to be shown in large amounts and in graphic portrayals, all with the approval of their internal review boards. (Verbal statement of industry critic)

Class Assignment. You are the marketing vice president of a major consumer products firm. What stand will you take concerning advertisements of your company's products on television programs that depict violence? Remember, those are among the most popular of the programming alternatives.

Footnotes

1. Dorothy Singer, "Caution: Television May Be Hazardous to a Child's Mental Health," *Developmental and Behavioral Pediatrics,* October 1989, p. 259.

2. *Statistical Abstract of the United States,* Editions 73, 81, 91, 101, and 114.

3. Leo Christensen, "Without Redeeming Social Value," in *Where Do You Draw the Line?* ed. Victor B. Cline (Provo, UT: Brigham Young University Press, 1974), p. 311.

4. Lynette Friedrich-Cofer, "Time for Research Is Past," *Media and Values* (Los Angeles: Media Action Research Center, Fall 1985), p. 6

5. *Industry Perspective on Television Violence,* 1983, p. 14

6. Victor Cline, *Where Do You Draw the Line?* (Provo, UT: Brigham Young University Press, 1975), p. 352.

Managerial Ethics and Normative Philosophy

The ethical dilemma in management centers on the continual conflict, or on the continual potential for that conflict, that exists between the economic and the social performance of an organization. Business firms have to operate profitably or they will not survive over the long term; that is their economic performance. Business firms also have to recognize their obligations to employees, customers, suppliers, distributors, stockholders, and the general public; that is their social performance. The problem—and the essence of the ethical dilemma in management— is that sometimes improvements in economic performance—increases in sales or decreases in costs—can be made only at the expense of one or more of the groups to whom the organization has some form of obligation. The economies of scale that follow a merger can be achieved only if the surplus employees are discharged or demoted. The efficiencies of direct factory-to-store distribution can be realized only if the existing wholesalers are replaced. The advantages of hydroelectric power can be realized only if a river valley is flooded and local residents are forced to move.

How do we decide when faced with these issues? How do we find the balance between economic performance and social performance that is "right" and "proper" and "just"? There are only three forms of analysis—ways of thinking about the dilemma and arriving at the "proper" balance—that can be used:

1. Economic analysis, based on impersonal market forces. The belief is that a manager should always act to maximize revenues and minimize costs, for this strategy, over the long term, will produce the greatest material benefits for society, and those benefits can be equitably distributed by political, not economic, means. As we saw, there are both practical and theoretical problems with that approach, so we cannot rely on economic analysis to resolve ethical conflicts; it certainly helps to know the financial revenues and costs, but something more is needed.

2. Legal analysis, based on impersonal social and political processes. The belief is that a manager should always act to obey the law, for the law within a democracy represents the collective moral judgment of members of society. Again, there are both practical and theoretical problems with that view, so we cannot rely on legal analysis, either by itself or in conjunction with economic analysis, to resolve ethical conflicts. It certainly helps to know the legality of a situation, but something even further is needed.

3. Philosophic analysis, based on rational thought processes. The view is that a manager should always act in accordance with either a single principle of behavior or a single statement of belief that is "right" and "proper" and "just" in and by itself. This is "moral reasoning": logically working from a first principle through to a decision on the duties we owe to others. There are some problems here also, though perhaps not as serious as in the other two instances.

Moral reasoning requires an understanding of normative philosophy. It is not possible to summarize normative philosophy in a single chapter—just as, quite frankly, it is not really possible to summarize micro-economic relationships or social/political processes in a single chapter—but it is possible to convey some of the basic concepts and methods, provided the reader is interested and willing to think about them. I assume that you are interested and willing to think about these issues or you would not have gotten this far.

DEFINITION OF NORMATIVE PHILOSOPHY

Philosophy is the study of thought and conduct. Normative philosophy is the study of the proper thought and conduct; that is, how we should behave. Normative philosophers have been looking at these issues for more than 2,400 years—since the time of Socrates, who lived from 470 to 399 B.C. They have attempted to establish a logical thought process, based upon an incontrovertible first principle, that would determine whether an act were "right" or "wrong," "good" or "evil," "fair" or "unfair." They have not been successful—otherwise all that would be needed would be to quote the sources and state the findings—but many of their concepts and methods are relevant to managerial ethics. All hard ethical decisions are compromises, between economic and social performance in the case of a business firm, between wants and duties in the case of an individual. Normative philosophy provides some help in making those compromises, but that help is not as extensive as one might wish. Here, then, is an introduction to the normative philosophy of morality and ethics.

First, there is a difference between morality and ethics. Morality refers to the standards of behavior by which people are judged, and particularly to the standards of behavior by which people are judged in their relationships with others. A person in the midst of a desert, isolated from anyone else, might act in a way that was immature, demeaning, or stupid, but he or she could not truly be said to have acted immorally since that behavior could have no impact upon others, unless it were to waste water or other resources needed by travelers in the future. Ethics, on the other hand, encompasses the system of beliefs that supports a particular view of morality. If I believe that a person should not smoke in a crowded room, it is because I have accepted the research findings of most scientists and the published statements of the Surgeon General that tobacco smoke is harmful; my acceptance of those findings is my ethic for that particular situation. Ethics is normally used in the plural form since most people have a system of interrelated beliefs rather than a single opinion. The difference between morality and ethics is easy to remember if one speaks of moral standards of behavior and ethical systems of belief, and I will use those terms in this discussion.

ETHICAL RELATIVISM

The next issue to be addressed in this description of the techniques of moral reasoning is that of ethical relativism. The question here is very basic: Are there objective universal principles upon which one can construct an ethical system of belief that is applicable to all groups in all cultures at all times? Moral standards of behavior differ between groups within a single culture, between cultures, and between times. This is obvious. For example, within the contemporary United States, moral standards for decisions on environmental protection differ between the leaders of public interest groups and the executives of major industrial corporations, and it is probable that these standards of environmental protection would differ even more greatly between the United States and Third World countries, or between the contemporary period and the late nineteenth century. The ethical systems of belief supporting those moral standards of behavior also differ; each group, in each country, in each time period, can usually give a very clear explanation of the basis for its actions. To continue the earlier example, representatives of natural resource interest groups can provide a perfectly logical reason for their support of a prohibition upon logging in old growth forests. Managerial personnel from a natural resource company can offer an equally logical reason for their opposition to such a prohibition. Both sides base their arguments on a system of beliefs as to what is best for the national society, but unfortunately those beliefs differ. I think we can all agree that among the most irritating aspects of the debate over ethical issues such as environmental protection are the attitudes of personal self-righteousness and the implications of opponent self-interest that seem to pervade all these discussions. Both sides assume that their systems of belief are so widely held, and so obviously logical, that their opponents have to be small-minded and illiberal; they do not recognize the legitimate differences that can exist between ethical systems as to what is "right" or "proper" or "good" for the country.

The question in ethical relativism is not whether different moral standards and ethical beliefs exist; they obviously do, and we all have experiences to confirm that fact. The question is whether there is any commonality that overrides the differences. In the mixed chorus of competing moral standards and diverse ethical systems, can we discern any single principle that unifies them all, or are we left with the weak and unsatisfactory conclusion that all ethical systems are equally valid, and that a person's choice has to be relative to his or her upbringing or education or position or country or culture? If all ethical systems are equally valid, then no firm moral judgments can be made about individual behavior, and we are all on our own, to do as we like to others, within economic and legal constraints.

Fortunately, there is one principle that does seem to exist across all groups, cultures, and times and that does form part of every ethical system; that is the belief that members of a group do bear some form of responsibility for the well-being of other members of that group. There is a widespread recognition that men and women are social beings, that cooperation is necessary for survival, and that some standards of behavior are needed to ensure that cooperation. In one of the most famous statements in ethical philosophy, Thomas Hobbes (1588–1679) argued that if everyone acted on the basis of his or her own self-interest and ignored the well-being of others, life would be "solitary, poor, nasty, brutish, and short."

People in all cultures, even the most primitive, do not act solely for their own self-interest, and people in those cultures understand that standards of behavior are needed to promote cooperation and ensure survival. These standards of behavior can be either negative—it is considered wrong to harm other members of the group—or positive—it is considered right to help other group members—but they do exist and can be traced in both sociological and anthropological studies. Consequently, the important question in moral relativism is not whether your moral standards are as good as mine; it is whether your moral standards that benefit society are as good as mine that benefit society.[1] The second question is very different from the first; it forces both of us to justify our standards relative to a principle that does extend over groups, cultures, and times. We can say that our definitions of what is "right" differ, and we can each act in accordance with those definitions and believe that we are morally correct; yet the way in which we determine what is "right" is exactly the same.

The fact that there can be two different moral standards, both of which can be considered to be "right," is confusing to many people. Let me try to clarify this apparent paradox with an example, and we will use the familiar example of the Brazilian customs. Let us say that I am from that South American country, and I believe it is morally acceptable to pay small bribes to the customs agents in order to expedite import clearance and shipment. You, on the other hand, are from the United States, and you find the practice to be morally unacceptable. We differ, though I work for you, in the same company, so I don't dwell on the differences. You come to Brazil; together we shepherd an important shipment through customs. You return to New York and tell your friends at lunch, "I had to pay." They are shocked, or would be if South American customs officials were not so notorious. I have dinner with friends that night, and tell them, "The man didn't want to pay." They are shocked, or would be if North American business practices were not often thought to be so bizarre. Both of us are right, as long as we base our standards on what we believe to be best for society. I think, "Customs agents need the money; our government sets their salary assuming that they make a small percentage"; you think, "The system would work better if everyone were much more honest." Both of our standards are based upon what we believe to be best for our society; consequently both are "right." Now, if we had the time and wanted to make the effort, we could search for a universal principle that would help us define what we meant by "best" for our society, and if we could measure that benefit, then we might be able to agree on which of our standards was more "right." What I am trying to explain, using this illustration, is that two different moral standards can both be believed "right"; that is not the same thing as saying that the two different moral standards are "right." We have to accept the proposition that we bear some responsibility for other members of our society or life becomes very "solitary, poor, nasty, brutish, and short," for us as well as for others. That responsibility becomes the absolute upon which our ethical systems are based.

This is somewhat in the nature of an aside, but the question of moral relativism—whether moral standards are valid across groups and cultures and times, or whether moral standards just depend upon individual and social and cultural circumstances—is sometimes applied to business firms. It is possible to think of business as a "game" in which different rules apply than in everyday life—a game similar to poker or dice in which no one expects the truth to be fully spoken or contracts to be fully honored.[2] Game strategy, it is said, requires exaggerations and concealments in making statements; the hearer has to be vigilant. Game outcome, it is alleged, encourages shortfalls in fulfilling contracts; the buyer has to be wary.

It is not difficult to find evidence of this "game" approach to business. Company-union wage negotiations are seldom examples of verisimilitude. Public accountants would not be needed if all financial figures were accurately reported. There is a reason that gas pumps and grocery scales are inspected by a public agency and sealed to prevent tampering.

What do you think of this view of management as a game, in which almost any act is permitted that the other side does not detect and offset, a game in which the rules are set by the players, using their moral standards, which are "fully as good as anyone else's"? How would you argue against this view? You should come back to the absolute of some responsibility for other members of society, which has been exhibited by every other culture at every other time, and you set the rule that their moral standards *that benefit society* are fully as good as anyone else's that benefit society. The standards of lying and cheating benefit only the liar and the cheater; if those standards are applied to everyone, the advantages disappear, and society becomes impossible, with no truth and no trust.

Given that you accept the basic premise that both you and I bear some form of responsibility for other people within our society, and that our society cannot continue to exist without some standards of behavior between individuals and groups, how do we determine whether those standards are "right" or "wrong"? We all have an intuitive understanding of right and wrong, but we don't know exactly how to classify our own actions, or those of our neighbors.

The universal recognition that we owe something to other people within our society, and that we are bound by a concept of right and wrong in our behavior to those people, has to be made operational. That is, we have to establish some consistent analytical method to classify our actions as "right" or "wrong." If we can't, it's not for lack of trying. As mentioned before, intellectual history over the past 2,400 years has been filled with attempts to justify moral standards and to establish ethical systems. None work perfectly, but there are five major systems that do have a direct relevance to managerial decisions: Eternal Law, Utilitarian Theory, Universalist Theory, Distributive Justice, and Personal Liberty.

ETERNAL LAW

Many church leaders and some philosophers (Thomas Aquinas and Thomas Jefferson among them) believe that there is an Eternal Law, incorporated in the mind of God, apparent in the state of Nature, revealed in the Holy Scripture, and immediately obvious to any man or woman who will take the time to study either nature or the Scripture. Thomas Jefferson, really the first of the secular humanists, believed that the truths of this law were "self-evident," in his famous phrase, that the rights were "inalienable," and that the duties could easily be derived from the rights. If people had rights to "life, liberty and the pursuit of happiness," then they had obligations to ensure those rights to others, even if this meant revolution against the British Crown. Religious leaders tend to emphasize the revealed source of the truth more than the reasoned nature, but they also believe that the state of the Law is unchanging, and that the rights and duties are obvious: if we are Loved, then we must love others.[3] This reciprocal exchange is summarized in Christian theology by the Golden Rule: Do unto others as you would have others do unto you.

What is wrong with Eternal Law or Natural Law, interpreted by either religious leaders or normative philosophers, as the basis for an ethical system in management? Nothing, except for the number of interpretations. No two Natural Law theorists, and very few religious writers, have ever been able to agree on the exact provisions of the revealed or reasoned truth. Each religion provides moral standards for their members, and many of the members observe those standards in daily life, but the standards differ between groups, and there is no way to determine which one is "right" or "best" or "proper" for the full society. Even the Golden Rule, that simple, elegant, sensible guide to life, can't somehow be applied universally. If you were a wealthy person, you would probably want others to retain their wealth, and you would expect to be treated the same way. If I were a poor person, I would wish others to share their income and benefits, just as I would be willing to share the little I had. Religious rules of conduct tend to be situation dependent; that is, our interpretation of them seems to vary with our personal circumstances. This may happen because most of our religious injunctions for moral behavior were developed many years ago in an agricultural society that had greater equality between individuals but less liberty for each person; the rules are not easily applied in an industrial society with those conditions exactly reversed.

UTILITARIANISM: A TELEOLOGICAL THEORY

The teleological approach to managerial ethics places complete emphasis upon the outcome, not the intent, of individual actions. Teleology is derived from a Greek term that means outcome or result, and some of the most influential philosphers in the Western tradition—including Jeremy Bentham and J. S. Mill—have held that the moral worth of personal conduct can be determined solely by the consequences of that behavior. That is, an act or decision is "right" if it results in benefits for people, and it is "wrong" if it leads to damages or harm; the objective obviously is to create the greatest degree of benefits for the largest number of people while incurring the least amount of damages or harm.

The benefits can vary. Material benefits are not the only ones that count, though they are certainly a good starting place for the calculations, but friendships, knowledge, health, and the other satisfactions we all find in life should be included as well. Think in terms of satisfactions, not pleasures; focusing on pleasures can lead to a very hedonistic and self-centered approach. The aggregate satisfactions or benefits for everyone within society have to be considered.

The benefits are not all positive. There are negative costs and adverse outcomes associated with each action, and they have to be included to establish a balance. The negative costs and adverse outcomes include pain, sickness, death, ignorance, isolation, and unhappiness. The aggregate harms or costs have to be considered, and then a balance of the net consequences can be computed.

This teleological ethical system—focusing on net consequences not individual intentions—is termed Utilitarianism, a philosophy originated by Jeremy Bentham (1748–1832), a British thinker. The name of the philosophy is derived from the word utility, which had an eighteenth-century meaning that referred to the degree of usefulness of a household object or a domestic animal; that is, a horse could be said to have a utility for plowing beyond the cost of its upkeep. Utility has this same meaning, and this same derivation, in microeconomic theory; it measures our degree of preference for a given good or service relative to price. In Utilitarian theory, the term refers to our perception of the net benefits and costs associated with a given act.

Utilitarianism is obviously close to the economic concept of cost/benefit analysis, particularly as the benefits are not to be confused with expediency and have to be calculated for the long-term consequences as carefully as for the short-term outcomes. Utilities, both benefits and costs, have to be computed equally for everyone. My satisfactions, and my costs, cannot be considered to be more important in some way than your satisfactions, and your costs. The decision rule that is then followed is to produce the greatest net benefits for society; an act is "right" if, and only if, it produces greater net benefits for society than any other act possible under the circumstances. There are of course problems in measuring net benefits—the combination of positive and negative outcomes associated with the act—but mathematical precision is not required; we can approximate the outcomes and include them in our calculations.

Utilitarianism differs from the economic concept of cost/ benefit analysis in that the distribution of the costs and benefits has to be included as well. That is, these are net benefits to society, and each individual within the society has to be considered equally, and treated equally in the distribution. "The greatest good for the greatest number" takes precedence in Utilitarian theory over "The greatest good for a smaller, more elite number."

To save time, and to avoid the need to compute the full consequences of every decision and action, most Utilitarians recommend the adoption of simplifying rules. These rules, such as "always tell the truth" or "never renege on a contract," can be logically shown to lead to beneficial outcomes in all foreseeable cases, but the basis for the rules remains the balance of positive and negative consequences that come from every act or decision.

What is wrong with Utilitarianism? Not very much, except for the possibility of exploitation. In the vast majority of cases, where no one is going to be hurt very badly, and particularly where it is possible to use financial equivalents for both the costs and the benefits, it is a familiar and useful form of analysis. But, there is always the possibility of justifying benefits for the great majority of the population by imposing sacrifices or penalties on a small minority. For example, substantial benefits could be brought to large numbers of the American people by expropriating all the property of the readers of the *Harvard Business Review*. This proposal, which might win the approval of a few truly liberal economists and a few extremely opportunistic politicians, would hopefully be rejected by all normative philosophers. Utilitarianism fails because in reality it is two principles: greatest good and greatest number; at some point in our decision processes on important matters, these two principles come into conflict, and then we have no single means of determining what is the "right" or "best" or "proper" act.

Lastly, Utilitarianism fails because we can probably all agree that there are some actions that are simply wrong, despite great apparent net benefits for a huge majority. Dostoevsky provided the extreme example. In *The Brothers Karamazov* he asked what should be done if the happiness of the whole human race, forever, could be brought about by the sacrifice of only one person, one completely innocent child, who would have to be tortured to death. No one should ever be able to accept that exchange. Teleological theory fails as a determinant of moral actions because it is impossible to balance the benefits of the majority against the sacrifices of a minority.

UNIVERSALISM: A DEONTOLOGICAL THEORY

The deontological approach to managerial ethics, in essence, is the reverse of teleological theory. Deontology is derived from another Greek term referring to the duties or the obligations of an individual. This ethical theory states that the moral worth of an action cannot be dependent upon the outcome because those outcomes are so indefinite and uncertain at the time the decision to act is made; instead, the moral worth of an action has to depend upon the intentions of the person making the decision or performing the act. If I wish the best for others, then my moral actions are praiseworthy, even though I happen to be an ineffectual and clumsy individual who always seems to be breaking something or hurting someone. It is assumed that we are not all clumsy and ineffectual people, and therefore that good intentions will normally result in beneficial outcomes.

Personal intentions can be translated into personal duties or obligations because, if we truly wish the best for others, then we will always act in certain ways to ensure beneficial results, and those ways become duties that are incumbent upon us rather than choices that are open to us. It is our duty to tell the truth; it is our duty to adhere to contracts; it is our duty not to take property that belongs to others. (Truthfulness, legality, and honesty can be logically derived from the basic principles of all ethical systems; in deontological theory they are duties we owe to others, while in teleological theory they are the actions that bring the greatest benefits to others.)

Our personal duties are universal, applicable to everyone, and consequently much of deontological theory is also termed Universalism, just as large portions of teleological theory are called Utilitarianism. The first duty of Universalism is to treat others as ends and not as means. Other people should be seen as valuable ends in themselves, worthy of dignity and respect, and not as impersonal means to achieve our own ends. No actions can be considered "right" in accordance with personal duty if it disregards the ultimate moral worth of any other human being.

Immanuel Kant (1724–1804) proposed a simple test for personal duty and goodwill, to eliminate self-interest and self-deception, and to ensure regard for the moral worth of others. The test is to ask yourself whether you would be willing to have everyone in the world, faced with similar circumstances, forced to act in exactly the same way. This is the Categorical Imperative; "categorical," of course, means absolute or unqualified, and the precept is that an act or decision can be judged to be "good" or "right" or "proper" only if everyone must, without qualification, perform the same act or reach the same decision, given similar circumstances.

Kant starts with the simple proposition that it is unfair for me to do something that others don't do or can't do or won't do. This is not because the total effect upon society might be harmful if everyone took the same action such as refusing to pay taxes—that would be a utilitarian doctrine based upon outcomes rather than a universalist precept based upon duties—but because I owe others the duty of acting consistently. I have a "will," or a view of the way I want the world to be, and my views must be consistent or I would have a "contradiction in wills," which is not fair to others given my duty to act rationally and consistently. That is, I pay taxes not because if everyone else did not pay taxes the government would collapse and there would be chaos, but because I want a world of law and order, and therefore I must also want to provide the financial support for that law and order. Law and order and taxes are right for me if, and only if, they are right for everyone else—that is, if they are "universalizable." Kant can be understood as an attempt to tie moral actions to rational decisions, with rationality defined as being based upon consistent and universal maxims. Moral standards, according to Kant, are based upon logical consistency.

The two formulations by Kant—(1) to act only in ways that I would wish all others to act, faced with the same set of circumstances, and (2) always to treat other people with dignity and respect—can be viewed as a single injunction. The first version says that what is morally right for me must be morally right for others. Everyone is of equal value. If this is so, then no person's rights should be subordinated to those of anyone else. If that is so, then we must treat people as free and equal in the pursuit of their interests.

Universalism, particularly when supported by the Categorical Imperative test, is a familiar and useful guide to behavior. The common law is a form of Universalism: Everyone, faced with a just debt, should pay that debt and no one, needing money, should rob banks. Company policies that have a legal or ethical content are usually Universalist: All personnel managers, in considering promotions and pay increases, should include length of service as well as individual ability; and no product manager, in setting prices, should contact competitors or agree to trade constraints.

What is wrong with Universalism? It is a useful method of moral reasoning, but there are no priorities and there are no degrees. I might will law and order to be absolute, with no opposition to the government outside of the formal electoral process, while you might prefer greater personal freedoms. I might will that everyone pay taxes at 7 percent of their annual income, while you might believe that a graduated income tax would be more equitable. Universalism is another ethical system that seems to be very dependent for interpretation upon the situation of the individual. Even the more basic formulation of the Categorical Imperative—to treat each other as moral objects, worthy of respect and dignity—provides very limited help. It is difficult to treat others as ends and not as means all the time, particularly when many serve as means to our personal ends: storekeepers are means of procuring our dinners; customers are means of earning our livelihoods; employees are means of staffing our factories. Both formulations of the Categorical Imperative have to be filled in with the Utilitarian principle—I should want some rule to be a universal law if the consequences of its adoption would be beneficial to others—or with some other values—justice, freedom, etc.—that summarize whole areas of moral conviction. But that principle and those values have to come from outside of the formal Universalist theory.

DISTRIBUTIVE JUSTICE

Neither of the two classical theories, Utilitarianism or Universalism, can be used to judge all moral actions under all circumstances, and consequently two modern ethical systems have been developed, based more upon values than upon principles. The first of these, the theory of Distributive Justice, has been proposed by John Rawls, a member of the Harvard faculty, and is explicitly based upon the primacy of a single value: justice. Justice is felt to be the first virtue of social institutions, as truth is the first virtue of systems of thought. A theory, however useful and complete, has to be rejected or revised if it is found to be untrue; in the same fashion our laws and institutions, no matter how efficient or accepted, must be reformed or abolished if they are unjust.

Professor Rawls proposes that society is an association of individuals who cooperate to advance the good of all. Therefore the society, and the institutions within that society, are marked by conflict as well as by collaboration. The collaboration comes about since individuals recognize that joint actions generate much greater benefits than solitary efforts; the conflict is inherent because people are concerned by the just distribution of those benefits. Each person prefers a greater to a lesser share and proposes a system of distribution to ensure that greater share. These distributive systems can have very different bases: to each person equally, or to each according to his or her need, to his or her effort, to his or her contribution, or to his or her competence. Most modern economic systems make use of all five principles: public education is, theoretically, distributed equally, while welfare payments are on the basis of need, sales commissions on the basis of effort, public honors on the basis of contribution, and managerial salaries on the basis of competence.

Professor Rawls believes that these assorted distributive systems are unjust. He suggests that the primacy of justice in the basic structure of our society requires greater equality, because free and rational persons, recognizing the obvious benefits of cooperation and concerned about the just distribution of those benefits, would accept social and economic inequalities only if they could be shown to result in compensating benefits for everyone, and particularly for the least advantaged members of society: poor, unskilled, and with native intelligence but no education or training. According to Rawls, I would not object to your having more of the social and economic benefits than I do, but I would object to working hard, beyond the minimum level of effort required to maintain my present standard of living, just so that you could have more. It is not hard to find evidence of this attitude within our society, so the theory of distributive justice does appear to have some empirical support.

Professor Rawls starts, however, not with our society, but with a "natural state," a hypothetical existence at the beginning of time when people were still ignorant of the exact nature of the differences among them—that is, when no one knew who was the most talented, the most energetic, the most competent. What reciprocal arrangement, he asks, would people under those conditions make for the just distribution of the benefits produced by their cooperation? This is the familiar idea of the social contract, and the basic question is, What principles would free and rational persons, concerned with furthering their own interests yet wishing to maintain their cooperative efforts, adopt as defining the fundamental terms of their association?

They would not select absolute equality in the distribution of benefits, Professor Rawls argues, because they would recognize that some of them would put forth greater efforts, have greater skills, develop greater competences, and so on. They would not agree to absolute inequality based upon effort, skill, or competence because they would not know who among them had those qualities and consequently who among them would receive the greater and the lesser benefits. Instead, they would develop a concept of conditional inequality, where differences in benefits had to be justified, and they would propose a rule that those differences in benefits could be justified only if they could be shown to result in compensating benefits for everyone, and in particular for the least advantaged members of their society. That is, the distribution of income would be unequal, but the inequalities would have to work for the benefit of all, and they could be shown to work for the benefit of all if it was obvious that they helped in some measure the least advantaged among us, those who were least able to influence events. If those people were helped in some measure, then it would seem clear that everyone else benefited to some extent as well, and then everyone would cooperate to produce even greater benefits.

Distributive Justice can be expanded from an economic system for the distribution of benefits to an ethical system for the evaluation of behavior in that acts can be considered to be "right" and "just" and "proper" if they lead to greater cooperation by members of our society, and "wrong" and "unjust" and "improper" if they lead in the opposite direction. What are the problems with this concept of distributive justice? It is entirely dependent upon an acceptance of the proposition that social cooperation provides the basis for all economic and social benefits. Individual effort is downplayed, if not ignored. We all recognize that some organized activities would never take place unless some one individual was willing to take the risks and responsibilities of starting and directing those activities. This individual effort is ignored in Distributive Justice: it forms the basis, however, for the fifth and last ethical system to be discussed.

CONTRIBUTIVE LIBERTY

The theory of Contributive Liberty (this phrase is my own, developed to contrast with Distributive Justice) is an ethical system proposed by Robert Nozick, also currently a member of the Harvard faculty. This system is another based upon the primacy of a single value, rather than a single principle, but that value is liberty rather than justice. Liberty is thought to be the first requirement of society. An institution or law that violates individual liberty, even though it may result in greater happiness and increased benefits for others, has to be rejected as being unjust.

Professor Nozick agrees that society is an association of individuals, and that cooperation between those individuals is necessary for economic gain, but he would argue that the cooperation comes about as a result of the exchange of goods and services. The holdings of each person, in income, wealth, and the other bases of self-respect, are derived from other people in exchange for some good or service, or are received from other people in the form of a gift. An existing pattern of holdings may have come about through application of any of the principles of distribution (to each equally, or to each according to need, effort, contribution, or competence), but those patterns will be changed by transfers, and those transfers, by exchange or gift, can be considered to be "just" as long as they are voluntary. Nonvoluntary exchanges, based upon the use of social force or other coercive means, are unjust.

Contributive Liberty can be expanded from essentially a market system for the exchange of holdings to an ethical system for the evaluation of behavior, because individuals must be allowed to make informed choices among alternative courses of action leading towards their own welfare, and these choices are "just" or "right" or "proper" as long as the same opportunities for informed choices are extended to others. Justice depends upon equal opportunities for choice and exchange, not upon equal allocations of wealth and income. What is wrong with this concept of liberty? It is based upon a very narrow definition of liberty that is limited to the negative right not to suffer interference from others; there may also be a positive right to receive some of the benefits enjoyed by others. That is, the right to life is certainly the right not to be killed by your neighbors, but it may also include the right to continue living through access to some minimal level of food, shelter, clothing, and medical assistance. And, it is assumed that the food, shelter, clothing, and medical assistance are produced through personal initiative, not through social cooperation.

CONCLUSIONS ON NORMATIVE PHILOSOPHY AS THE BASIS FOR MORAL CHOICE

There are five major ethical systems, as summarized in Exhibit 4–1. They do not outwardly conflict with each other—an action such as lying that is considered immoral in one system will generally be considered immoral in all the other systems—but they cannot be reconciled into a logically consistent whole, for eventually conflict will arise over the primacy of the alternative principles and values. Each ethical system expresses a portion of the truth. Each system has adherents and opponents. And each, it is important to admit, is incomplete or inadequate as a means of judging the moral content of individual actions or decisions. What does this mean to managers? I would suggest that there is one major and direct implication for managers, and three more minor or indirect consequences for organizations, that come from the incomplete nature of ethical systems.

Exhibit 4–1

Summary of Beliefs and Problems in the Five Major Ethical Systems

	Nature of Ethical Belief	*Problems in the Ethical System*
Eternal Law	Moral standards are given in an Eternal Law, which is revealed in Scripture or apparent in nature and then interpreted by religious leaders or humanist philosophers; the belief is that everyone should act in accordance with the interpretation.	There are multiple interpretations of the Law, but no method to chose among them beyond human rationality, and human rationality needs an absolute principal or value as the basis for choice.
Utilitarian Theory	Moral standards are applied to the outcome of an action or decision; the principle is that everyone should act to generate the greatest benefits for the largest number of people.	Immoral acts can be justified if they provide substantial benefits for the majority, even at an unbearable cost or harm to the minority; an additional principle or value is needed to balance the benefit-cost equation.
Universalist Theory	Moral standards are applied to the intent of an action or decision; the principle is that everyone should act to ensure that similar decisions would be reached by others, given similar circumstances.	Immoral acts can be justified by persons who are prone to self-deception or self-importance, and there is no scale to judge between "wills"; additional principle or value is needed to refine the Categorical Imperative concept.
Distributive Justice	Moral standards are based upon the primacy of a single value, which is justice. Everyone should act to ensure a more equitable distribution of benefits, for this promotes individual self-respect, which is essential for social cooperation.	The primacy of the value of justice is dependent upon acceptance of the proposition that an equitable distribution of benefits ensures social cooperation.
Personal Liberty	Moral standards are based upon the primacy of a single value, which is liberty. Everyone should act to ensure greater freedom of choice, for this promotes market exchange, which is essential for social productivity.	The primacy of the value of liberty is dependent upon acceptance of the proposition that a market system of exchange ensures social productivity.

The major implication for managers is that there is no single system of belief, with rationally derived standards of moral behavior or methods of moral reasoning, that can guide executives fully in reaching "proper" ethical decisions when confronting difficult moral problems. A moral problem, to repeat the earlier definition and sharpen the present discussion, is one that will harm others in ways that are beyond their own control. A decision to introduce a new brand of chocolate cake mix has no moral dimensions since others within the society are perfectly free to buy or to ignore the product. But a decision to close the plant producing the cake mix, or to use a high-cholesterol shortening in the production of that mix, or to ask for government help in shutting off imports competitive to that mix, would have a moral content, since these issues do have an impact upon others. A product manager, faced let us say in an unlikely but perhaps not totally unrealistic problem of imported cake mixes from a foreign country that has very low wage rates and very high government subsidies, has to respond, and each response has moral implications. Lowering production means cutting employment; reducing the cost means compromising the quality; and requesting government help means endorsing trade restrictions.

There is no single system of belief to guide managers in reaching "proper" ethical decisions to difficult moral problems, but this does not mean that all of us are on our own, to do as we like in our decisions and actions that affect others. We do have obligations to other people. We cannot ignore those obligations. The difficulty comes in identifying our obligations and then in evaluating our alternatives, with no single set of moral standards to guide us.

What should we do? Instead of using just one ethical system, which we must admit is imperfect, we have to use all five systems and think through the consequences of our actions on multiple dimensions. Does a given decision result in greater benefits than damages for society as a whole, not just for our organization as part of that society? Is the decision self-serving, or would we be willing to have everyone else take the same action when faced with the same circumstances? We understand the need for social cooperation; will our decision increase or decrease the willingness of others to contribute? We recognize the importance of personal freedom; will our decision increase or decrease the liberty of others to act? Lastly, we know that the universe is large and infinite, while we are small and our lives are short; is our personal improvement that important, measured against the immensity of that other scale?[4]

Moral reasoning of this nature, utilizing all five ethical systems, is not simple and easy, but it is satisfying. It does work. It works particularly well when combined with economic and legal analysis. That combination will be the topic of the next chapter, Managerial Ethics and Individual Decisions.

Footnotes

1. For a more complete discussion of the very basic question of ethical relativism, see Richard Brand, *Ethical Theory* (New York: Prentice-Hall, 1959).

2. Albert Carr, in a controversial article titled "Is Business Bluffing Ethical?" (*Harvard Business Review,* January–February 1968) suggested that business is a game, and that it is necessary only to follow the rules of the game, not personal moral standards.

3. It seems awkward to discuss the philosophic basis of religious belief in a book on management, but religious beliefs do have an impact upon managers as well as upon others and should be included in any description of ethical systems.

4. Once again I am faced with the problem of discussing religious beliefs in a book on management, with the added complexity of recognizing that these beliefs differ among the major religious groups in the United States. Rather than use the moral standards of one group as representative of all others, I prefer to refer to the immensity of the concept of an Eternal Law and let each faith infer its own standards based upon an interpretation of that Law.

CASE 4–1

Conflict of Duties in Marketing

The managers of a business firm obviously have duties to their stockholders who are the owners of the company and benefited by its profits. The managers also have duties to their stakeholders who are the people associated with the company in some way and affected by its actions. These two sets of duties frequently come into conflict. One of the basic moral responsibilities of management is to resolve those conflicts in ways that can be considered to be "right" and "just" and "fair." How would you resolve the following five conflicts in the functional area of marketing; all of these actions were legal at the time they were proposed or considered:

1. *Cash payments.* Many of the large supermarket chains now demand substantial cash payments from their suppliers before agreeing to stock new products. These payments are called "stocking fees" or "shelving costs." Supermarket managers claim that they do not know whether a new consumer food product will be successful or not before they put it on their shelves, and consequently they want to be reimbursed for the expenses involved before they accept it for retail sale. The payments go to the chains (they are not bribes paid to the purchasing agents), but they are in addition to the price discounts that are standard in the food distribution industry, and they are not small. Forty percent of the value of the first shipment is not uncommon. Large and well financed suppliers such as Procter & Gamble or General Mills have no difficulty in making those payments, and they recover the amounts through somewhat higher consumer prices at the start. Small and entrepreneurial food products companies find it very difficult to pay the required amounts and are, in essence, shut out of the supermarkets. Is it "right" for supermarket chains to charge stocking fees to large and small companies alike? What do the executives in those chains "owe" to their suppliers?

2. *Distributor changes.*   Many manufacturers of both consumer and industrial products are streamlining their operations and cutting their costs in an attempt to meet foreign and domestic competition. Wholesale distribution is an obvious target for these cost cutting efforts. Often, either as a result of a recent merger or acquisition that increased sales volume or following a review of alternative transportation routes that showed reduced expenses, a manufacturer will find that it is less costly to establish regional warehouses and then sell direct to retail stores and dealers rather than to rely any longer on wholesale distributors. Distributors usually have only a "shake-of-the-hand" contract with the manufacturers they represent that can legally be broken on 60 days' notice "with or without cause". The distributors, however, generally claim that they have a lengthy history of cooperation with the manufacturer dating back 20, 30, or even 50 years, and that they had helped in the past to build the products and expand the sales of the manufacturer, and should not be discarded so quickly now. Is it "right" for manufacturing firms to terminate a wholesaler who has performed well in the past just because it is less costly to sell direct today? What do the executives in those firms "owe" to their distributors?

3. *Special discounts.*   Airlines and hotel chains have recently begun negotiating special rates for large corporations that are, of course, large users of their services. Special rates on the airlines for these customers are said to be 32% below the fares for the advance purchase coach tickets available to everyone else, though without the restrictions for advanced purchases or weekend stay-overs that are applied to others. Special rates at the hotel chains for large corporate customers are said to average 22% less than those assigned to members of the general public. The reason for these special rates is clear; it is to compete for the business of the large corporations that account for 60% of all travel expenditures in the U.S. Legally it is permissible for suppliers to offer special rates for goods or services to large corporations if it can be shown that those rates reflect economies of scale in providing the goods and services. Small business management associations and travel agency trade groups claim that those economies of scale do not exist in air travel and hotel accommodations because the reservations are made and the services are provided for individuals or small groups, not for large numbers of people at one time, and that consequently the charges should be equal for all. Is it "right" for airlines and hotel chains to provide special low rates for their large customers that are not made available to small companies or the general public? What do the executives at these firms owe to their smaller customers who have limited power to exert demands?

4. *Incomplete advertisements.*   Many insurance companies offer "guaranteed" life insurance to elderly persons through advertisements that feature well-known television personalities (Dick Van Dyke, Ed Asner, Art Linkletter, etc). The advertisements stress the peace of mind that comes from having enough insurance to pay funeral expenses and leave a small inheritance to family members. The policies are said in the ads to be guaranteed because an applicant cannot be rejected because of age or illness and because the rates will not be increased over time. The advertisements do not explain that the rates for these guaranteed policies are 100% to 200% higher than the rates for people of equivalent age who do submit to medical exams to determine their fitness, and that no payments will be made for death during the first two years of coverage. Is it "right" for insurance companies to promote policies without full disclosure of comparative prices and "small print" terms? What do the executives at these firms "owe" to older customers who are not as careful in detecting fraud or exploitation?

  5. *Inaccurate advertisements.* Many television advertisements for consumer products are grossly inaccurate if not deliberately untruthful. Cold and flu remedies promise "24-hour relief". Frozen foods ads show colorful pictures of meals that have been prepared in a restaurant rather than taken from the package. Airlines appeals portray passenger accommodations with much greater space across seats and between rows than is ever found on the actual commercial flights. Is it "right" for television and magazine ads to misrepresent the appearance or exaggerate the perfor mance of their products? What do the executives at consumer product firms "owe" to their customers who have neither the time nor the resources to investigate claims?

Class Assignment. Decide what you believe is "owed" to each group of stakeholders in this series of problems.

CASE 4–2

Sarah Goodwin

Sarah Goodwin was a graduate of an MBA program on the West Coast. She had majored in marketing, was interested in retailing, and had been delighted to receive a job offer from a large and prestigious department store chain in northern California. The first year of employment at this chain was considered to be a training program, but formal instruction was very limited. Instead, after a quick tour of the facilities and a welcoming speech by the president, each of the new trainees was assigned to work as an assistant to a buyer in one of the departments. The intent was that the trainees would work with five or six buyers during the year, rotating assignments every two months, and would make themselves "useful" enough during those assignments so at least one buyer would ask to have that person join his/her department on a permanent basis.

Buyers are critical in the management of a department store. They select the goods to be offered, negotiate purchase terms, set retail prices, arrange displays, organize promotions, and are generally responsible for the operations of the departments within the store. Each buyer acts as a profit center, and sales figures and profit margins are reported monthly to the senior executives. In this particular chain, the sales and profits were calculated on a square foot basis (that is, per square foot of floor space occupied by the department), and the buyers contended, generally on a friendly basis, to outperform each other so that their square footage would be expanded. The buyers received substantial commissions, based upon monthly profits.

Sarah's first assignment was to work for the buyer of the gourmet food department. This was a small unit at the main store that sold packaged food items such as jams and jellies, crackers and cookies, cheese and spreads, candies, etc., most of which were imported from Europe. The department also offered preserved foods such as smoked fish and meats, and some expensive delicacies such as caviar, truffles, and estate-bottled wines. Many of the items were packaged as gifts, in boxes or baskets, with decorative wrapping and ties.

Sarah was originally disappointed to have been sent to such a small and specialized department, rather than to a larger one that dealt with more general fashion goods, but she soon found that this assignment was considered to be a "plum." The buyer, Maria Castellani, was a well-known personality throughout the store; witty, competent and sarcastic, she served as a sounding board, consultant, and friend to the other buyers. She would evaluate fashions, forecast trends, chastise managers ("managers" in a department store are the people associated with finance, personnel, accounting, or planning, not merchandising) and discuss retailing events and changes in an amusing, informative way. Everybody in the store seemed to find a reason to stop by the gourmet food department at least once during each day to chat with Maria. Sarah was naturally included in these conversations, and consequently she found that she was getting to know all of the other buyers, and could ask one of them to request her as an assistant at the next rotation of assignments.

For the first five weeks of her employment, Sarah was exceptionally happy, pleased with her career and her life. She was living in a house, on one of the cable car lines, with three other professionally employed women. She felt that she was performing well on her first job, and making sensible arrangements for her next assignment. Then, an event occurred that threatened to destroy all of her contentment:

We had received a shipment of thin little wafers from England that had a creme filling flavored with fruit: strawberries and raspberries. They were very good. They were packaged in foil covered boxes, but somehow they had become infested with insects.

We did not think that all of the boxes were infested, because not all of the customers brought them back. But, some people did, and obviously we could not continue to sell them. We couldn't inspect the packages, and keep the ones that were not infested, because there were too many—about $9,000 worth—and because we would have had to tear the foil to open each box. Maria said that the manufacturer would not give us a refund because the infestation doubtless occurred during shipment, or even during storage at our own warehouse.

Maria told me to get rid of them. I thought that she meant for me to arrange to have them taken to the dump, but she said, "Absolutely not. Call (name of an executive) at (name of a convenience store chain in southern California). They operate down in the ghetto, and can sell anything. We've got to get our money back."

Class Assignment.   What would you do in this situation? Make a set of specific recommendations for Sarah Goodwin.

CASE 4–3

Wal-Mart Stores in Northern Michigan

Wal-Mart Stores, Inc. in 1994 was the world's largest retailer, operating a chain of modern discount stores throughout the United States and beginning to expand abroad. It had started as a single shop selling work clothes and household items in Bentonville, Arkansas in 1969, but grew rapidly to the present total of 2,136 stores handling a wide variety of consumer goods. The average annual return to the shareholders since the 1980 listing on the New York Stock Exchange has been 32%; $10,000 invested at that time would today be worth $487,560. The founder, Sam Walton, who was known for his "folksy" approach to employees, customers, and stockholders alike, and who drove a pick-up truck to work through all those years of growth, was the wealthiest person in the United States at the time of his death in 1993.

The success of the Wal-Mart chain has been extensively studied, and its outstanding financial performance is said to be based upon six strategic concepts which combined to produce large sales volumes and low operating costs at each of the stores:

• Wide selection. The typical Wal-Mart carries over 35,000 items, about 35% more than the number handled by other discount chains such as K-Mart or Meijers.

• Low pricing. The typical Wal-Mart has a price structure that is 3 to 5 lower than other discount chains, and 15 to 25 below family owned stores. Family owned stores often cannot buy products at the prices charged by Wal-Mart.

• Niche placement. The typical Wal-Mart store is located in a rural community, with low taxes, wages, and land costs, but then draws upon a large 30 mile radius.

• Accurate data. Wal-Mart was the first national retailer to design and then build an on-line, real-time information system for prompt sales analysis and inventory control. They had accurate sales and inventory data, by store.

• Direct shipment. Wal-Mart shares their sales and inventory data by store with their suppliers, who then arrange for direct re-stocking without intermediate warehousing.

• Central purchasing. Wal-Mart purchases all items for all stores through a central buying unit that offers long-term large-scale contracts in return for very low prices.

The large selections and low prices bring customers from relatively wide distances, and consequently Wal-Mart generally develops a strip mall with a large grocery store as the other "anchor" tenant and fast food restaurants and specialty shops selling noncompeting items in between the two main stores, to both concentrate shoppers at a "one-stop" location and collect rents from the other merchants. The strip mall is generally built as an interconnected line of single story concrete block buildings with bare steel-truss roofs, containing from 250,000 to 360,000 square feet of selling space, and surrounded by 12 to 15 acres of asphalted parking lots and illuminated advertising signs. The resultant mall is huge. It is cheap. It may be unattractive but it is efficient. And, it is often resisted by local people for all four of those reasons.

The resistance is concentrated, of course, among the local merchants in the downtown areas of the local communities who will lose business to the new complex, if it is built. The local merchants are often joined by property owners and vacation visitors who are worried about the appearance of the mall and its impact upon their traditional "small town" way of life. Together, these groups make the following points in their argument:

• The downtown section will be "ruined" as the small locally owned stores have to close; they simply cannot compete against the huge economies of scale and scope of the Wal-Mart chain.

• The landscape will also be "ruined"; the flat design of the buildings, the low cost of the construction, and the great expanse of the parking at a new mall simply don't belong in an attractive rural setting.

• The vacation appeal may not be ruined, but certainly will be harmed; people don't want to drive hundreds of miles to find the same urban sprawl they left behind.

• The tax base will be altered; downtown businesses typically pay a large percentage of the local taxes. Once they close the burden shifts to the home owners and renters, not to the low cost mall.

• The job base will also be altered; downtown businesses and vacation resorts provide most of the local employment. Changes in the total in either category can be disastrous for the community.

The traditional response of Wal-Mart has been that they provide lower prices and better selections for local consumers, who are consequently much better off, and that the taxes they pay and the jobs they offer more than make up for whatever taxes and jobs are lost when local businesses close. Wal-Mart does not dispute that local businesses will close; their avowed aim is to dominate local retailing within every area in which they operate. In the few instances where that has not happened, Wal-Mart has simply closed the store and abandoned the mall. Numerous economic studies have confirmed the probable retail dominance; a new Wal-Mart strip mall will generally result in the closing of 35 to 40 local businesses within two to three years, which usually are boarded up rather than replaced. Those same economic studies show that the Wal-Mart strip mall does not quite make up for employment and tax losses, falling about 20 to 25% behind in both categories, also within the first two to three years.

A number of citizen groups in Petoskey, Michigan have been particularly adamant in opposing a recently announced plan by Wal-Mart to build a large (360,000 square foot of retail space) mall on 67 acres of farmland the company owns adjacent to Route 131, the southern entrance into town. Petoskey is an old and picturesque village or town situated directly on the shore of Lake Michigan, about 30 miles south of the Straits of Mackinac at the top of the lower peninsula.

Petoskey was originally the site of a trading post and mission school for the Indians. Development was slow until the arrival of the railroad in 1870. During the next 25 years Petoskey grew rapidly as a resort area, due to the inherent attractiveness of the region, easily reached by lake streamers or passenger trains from Grand Rapids, Kalamazoo, and Chicago. By 1895 there were 24 hotels and boarding houses, together with a thriving business district, all built with distinctive red brick architecture. The Methodist Church, which had run the mission school, converted their property to an educational camp for families, and added numerous cottages, lecture halls, concert facilities, and a downtown park along the waterfront. Gaslights installed at this time still operated in 1994. Restaurants and shops were intermingled and customers tended to stroll the downtown area in the evening in an evocation of earlier days in small town America.

Some factories for food processing—the climate and soil close to the shore have long been known for producing superior fruits and vegetables—and furniture manufacturing using hardwood from the nearby forests were started in the southern part of the town in the early 1900s, but those had mostly closed by the latter half of the century. A very small K-Mart had been built in one of the abandoned factories, but Wal-Mart had refused to consider that as an alternative due to the lack of parking, the inadequate space for product display, and the inherent inefficiency caused by older, multiple storied buildings.

Petoskey in 1995 was a prosperous, attractive town with a year-round population of 3,500 people that served as the trading center for Emmet County, which had a permanent population of 23,700 more. There were also 15,200 summer residents who owned property within the county, primarily along the shore, close to Petoskey. The area was almost totally dependent upon tourism during both the summer and winter; numerous golf courses and ski areas had been built close to the lake during the 1960s and 1970s, and these facilities attracted a constant stream of visitors.

Technically it was illegal for Wal-Mart to build upon the farmland that they owned, which had been zoned for farm, residential, and "light" commercial use. No one had ever anticipated that a mall might be built on that site, though it was one of the few that was flat enough for commercial construction within the region, and consequently the zoning restrictions were lenient, to make it easier for local farmers to survive. Courts, however, tended to interpret "light" commercial use broadly, and Wal-Mart was known for aggressive legal tactics, using large numbers of corporate attorneys in continuous hearings, suits, and appeals to simply override opposition. Small towns did not have the resources to oppose that effort. Vermont did successfully oppose Wal-Mart's entry into scenic or historic areas, but there zoning restrictions are both set and upheld by the state, not by the community.

Surveys of the Petoskey and Emmet County population bases have brought mixed results. A market research study conducted by an agency for Wal-Mart found that 47% of permanent residents in Petoskey and 73% of permanent residents in Emmet County approved of the concept of a new discount store for the obvious reasons: wider selections and lower prices; 89% of the summer residents in Emmet County opposed the idea. The opposition took photographs of an existing Wal-Mart strip mall in southern Michigan and of the boarded up central shopping district in that same town five years after the mall opened, displayed 8' × 12' enlargements of those photos in the lakeside park of Petoskey under the printed question "Do you want this urban sprawl in our town?" and garnered 22,000 signatures opposing the project over a three week period.

Class Assignment.   You are the Michigan district manager for Wal-Mart. Petoskey is one of the few remaining "untapped" areas in the state; the nearest Wal-Mart stores are 45 to 60 miles away, at Gaylord to the east or Mackinac City to the north. At both locations store closings and the decay of the central business district did follow the introduction of the discount chain; neither, however, is a tourist destination so that the impact upon tourism can't really be measured and then applied to Petoskey. You have just received the appeal, signed by 22,000 people, saying "Please don't destroy our town; we love it just the way it is." What do you do, and why?

CHAPTER 5

Managerial Ethics
and Individual Decisions

We have looked at economic analysis, legal analysis, and philosophical analysis as means of resolving ethical dilemmas, and have found that none are completely satisfactory; that none give us a method of deciding upon a course of action that we can say with certainty is "right" and "proper" and "fair " when attempting to find a balance between the economic and the social performance of an organization.

Economic analysis was the first to be investigated. The concept of impersonal market forces helping us to reach Pareto Optimality is appealing—all we have to do, then, is to maximize revenues and minimize costs, and the product markets, factor markets and political decisions will together eliminate or correct the harm or damages we cause to others— but there are both practical and theoretical problems with microeconomic theory. We have to admit that the markets are not all that efficient, and that the voters are not all that generous, and that consequently we cannot rely exclusively on economic analysis.

Legal analysis was the next to be considered. The concept of impersonal social processes is also appealing—all we have to do is to obey the law and we can feel that we are meeting the collective moral standards of a majority of our fellow citizens—but that concept also falls apart as we look at the process by which individual norms, beliefs, and values are institutionalized into the legal framework. We have to recognize that there are too many steps, and too many compromises, between individual moral standards and national legal requirements to reach a true consensus, and that consequently we cannot rely exclusively on legal analysis.

Philosophical analysis was the last to be reviewed. The concept of personal rational analysis is appealing—all we have to do is base our decisions upon a single principle (beneficiency or consistency) or upon a single value (justice or freedom)—but rational moral reasoning also has an internal flaw. If we attempt to use any one of the principles or any one of the values in moral reasoning, we find that we have to add a second principle or a second value to reach a logical conclusion. We have to accept that a combination of conflicting principles or values is not rational, and that consequently we cannot rely exclusively on philosophical analysis.

What do we do, then? How do we decide, when faced with an ethical dilemma that contrasts economic performance and social performance? We are forced to use all three methods of analysis.

We are forced to say to ourselves that if one of our decisions or actions generates an adequate financial return, conforms to current law, provides substantial benefits to a large number of people, is an action we can wish that everyone else would take, faced with the same set of alternatives and background factors, is "just" in the sense of increasing the potential for social cooperation, and is "equitable" in the sense of expanding the ability of others to choose for themselves, then we can say that decision or action is "right" and "proper" and "good."

Granted, this form of multiple analysis is complex. It would be better if we had a single decision rule that we could follow every time, but we don't. Does multiple analysis work? Yes, I think that it does. Let me show that it does by following through two examples of foreign bribery, one of which I think most of us would agree to be "wrong" and the other of which I think most of us would agree to be "permissible" if not "right," and see if multiple analysis helps us to understand these intuitive beliefs. If a means of analysis helps us to understand our intuitive beliefs—based upon our personal moral standards—when confronting a reasonably simple ethical problem, then I think that we can place greater reliance upon it when we don't have clear intuitive feelings and we face a much more complex ethical issue.

ETHICAL ANALYSIS AND THE LOCKHEED BRIBERY CASE

The first example—and the one that I think we can agree to be intuitively "wrong"—is that of Lockheed, and the payment of $3.8 million by the Lockheed Aircraft Corporation to various governmental officials and representatives of the prime minister in Japan to ensure the purchase of twenty TriStar passenger planes. This event was extensively reported, following testimony before a Congressional investigating committee, and Mr. Carl Kotchian, the president of Lockheed, has written an account of the conditions that led him to decide to pay the bribes. In his defense, I think that we have to understand that Mr. Kotchian did not leave for Japan carrying the corporate checkbook and a ballpoint pen; in essence he was forced into the payments.

Mr. Kotchian was directly responsible for the negotiations that led to the sale of the TriStar planes. However, he did not speak Japanese, and had to rely on advice and representations from the executives of a Japanese trading company that had been retained to act as the agent for

Lockheed. I think that we can assume that Mr. Kotchian had been prepared by his staff for the personal nature of Japanese business decisions on large-scale investments, which is a corollary of the consensus nature of Japanese business decisions on operating problems—after all, if product design and manufacturing method decisions are made by a group on the lower levels of the organization, the pattern will be established for strategic and investment decisions to be made by a group on the upper levels. I think that we can also assume that Mr. Kotchian had been warned by his staff of the interlocking structure of Japanese business firms and governmental agencies. But, no westerner can be fully prepared for the intricate maneuvering which this combination of group decision-making and interlocking organizational structures can generate.

These maneuvers, which Mr. Kotchian described as "Byzantine" in their complexity, extended over a period of 70 days. While Mr. Kotchian waited in a hotel room in downtown Tokyo, he was exposed to hurried meetings, intentional delays, midnight telephone calls, and continual intimations that the decision was at hand. Being a foreigner, and acting as a salesman, Mr. Kotchian was excluded from the decision process. The agents retained by Lockheed could meet with the prime minister at his private home, for breakfast, but the president of Lockheed could meet only with the technical and functional representatives of the airlines, who might advise but could not decide upon the purchase. These meetings, delays, and telephone calls were played out against a backdrop of a declining order backlog and a deteriorating competitive position for the company. Lockheed had failed over the prior two years to obtain orders from Alitalia, Lufthansa, and Sabena, in Europe, and a large foreign order was needed to bring unit sales above the breakeven volume and repay the engineering expense. The agents for Lockheed calmly assumed that "pledges" would be made, and explained that payments would be required, to ensure the sale of twenty planes to Nippon, in Japan. Perhaps Mr. Kotchian wondered, as he sat in that hotel room waiting for the next meeting or the next telephone call, if other aircraft suppliers had made those pledges in Europe, for the TriStar was an acceptable design, certainly equal to the competition. Probably Mr. Kotchian worried about the future of his company; the loss of the Nippon order, for more than $430 million in total revenues, would mean the forfeiture of sales momentum, the slowdown of design projects, and the discharge of production workers. He decided, and let us credit him with considerable worry and concern in that decision, to make the pledges and pay the bribes.

It is certainly easy for everyone now to condemn the decision by Mr. Kotchian to pay $3.8 million to government officials in Japan. It is much harder for most people to say that, faced with the same conditions of personal isolation, factual uncertainty, and corporate responsibility, they would not have reached the same decision. The presence of the mixed outcomes— political payoffs in Tokyo resulted in full employment in Burbank,

California—and the career implications—Mr. Kotchian did not mention the possibility in his account, but it certainly has to be recognized that he would probably have been replaced as president had Lockheed lost the fourth foreign order in a row—in this instance complicate the moral dilemma. If blame is to be ascribed, and it has to be in this instance for here the bribery payments were blatant, dishonest, and large, then members of the corporate staff should bear at least part of the responsibility for they had failed to advise Mr. Kotchian of the likelihood of payoff demands so that other alternatives could be considered in advance. It is hard to think of options when demands for very substantial amounts of money are presented in a matter-of-fact manner by high government officials, with the obvious endorsement and approval of the agents for your own firm.

I have tried to describe the bribe payment by Lockheed in a reasonably sympathetic light, giving some of the extenuating circumstances, but—as I stated previously—I assume that most of us agree that that payment was wrong. Why do we feel that way? Let us work through the multiple forms of analysis, and see if we can substantiate our feelings.

Economically, the order was large, at $430 million. We doubtless could compute the potential profit based upon published income and expense data for prior years, but that does not seem necessary; we recognize that the order would have resulted in a substantial profit. Legally, the bribe was not unlawful; this payment was one of those acts that led to the passage of the Foreign Corrupt Practices Act, but at the time Mr. Kotchian faced the decision, payments to foreign nationals were not contrary to U.S. law. In utilitarian terms—greatest good for the greatest number—we can partially excuse the payment: the benefits of employment in Burbank are very immediate and very obvious, while the damages to the democratic process in Japan are not as obvious, and quite diffused. It is in universalistic terms—everyone faced with the same set of circumstances must act in the same way—that we find definite support for our intuitive beliefs. Could we ever propose a rule that every president of a large company, faced with the potential loss of a critical order, should offer to pay 0.8% of the face value of that order as a bribe? In terms of justice—each act must benefit in some way the least advantaged amongst us—we definitely benefit only the most wealthy citizens of Japan. In terms of liberty—each act must help others to select their own course of action—we definitely restrict the ability of Japanese citizens to choose freely for themselves. I think that this multiple form of analysis leads us strictly to agree: the payment was "wrong."

ETHICAL ANALYSIS AND A JUSTIFIABLE BRIBERY CASE

Now, let us look at a bribe that I think most of us can say was certainly "permissible" if not absolutely "right." This example may be apocryphal, but it is another story that, if not true, should be. I have been told that after the passage of the Foreign Corrupt Practices Act in 1977, the board of directors of a large engineering and construction firm, with worldwide operations, decided that they would not only obey the law, they would enforce it. They set a limit of $50 that could be paid for minor services received, such as customs clearance or vehicle registration, in countries where it was customary to make those payments and where the salaries of the officials were low enough to indicate a general knowledge and acceptance of those payments. Higher payments for services were forbidden, and all payments for contract approval or sales assistance were banned. To convey this message, a group of senior executives was selected to visit each of the construction sites and supply depots. These were older men, with extensive field experience, and they were known and respected by the area managers, site supervisors, and job foremen. At each site or depot, the personnel were assembled, and the executives stated clearly, "You will not pay bribes above the stated limit, and those only for services where it is both customary and known. If you do make payments, either directly or indirectly, for amounts above $50 you will be discharged, despite your length of service, with no corporate sympathy, no retirement benefits, and no severance pay. We are going to run this company the way it should be run, with high quality work and absolute financial integrity. If that is not enough, and if we can't obtain engineering and construction contracts based upon that combination, we will close the company."

The message was heard, probably with mixed reactions but doubtless with complete clarity, by the personnel at all but a few of the overseas locations. Coming back from a remote site in the tropics, the pilot of the local airline taxied to the end of the runway, parked under the broiling sun, turned off the motors and air conditioning, and announced that he would take off after he had received a gift of $1,200 for his daughter's wedding. The money was paid, but the executives returned to New York, for they felt that they could no longer support an authoritative policy on corrupt practices which they had been unable to obey.

My opinion is that it is unfortunate that they discontinued their mission, for this is the most justifiable instance of bribery I know. I assume that most of you would agree. Why do we feel this way, and how can we rationalize our beliefs? Economically, the impact of the payment upon the performance of the firm was minimal, so we can disregard that form of analysis. Legally, we will have to admit that the payment was unlawful, for this event occurred after the passage of the Foreign Corrupt Practices Act, but we saw in the chapter on the rule of law that legal requirements often do not represent moral standards, and that seems to me to be the case here. From the utilitarian point of view, I would think that the greatest good for the greatest number would come from the bribe payment, for otherwise the senior executives faced extreme discomfort and eventual illness in the stifling metal cabin of a grounded airplane, and the cost was minimal to others. From the universalist point of view, I should hope that we could agree that everyone condemned to this situation should be free to make the payment. The bribe does not decrease any opportunities for social cooperation, and it does increase the executives' ability to choose freely for themselves in the future, after release from the plane. I am not saying that I think that the extortion of the bribe by the aircraft pilot was in any way defensible, but I do believe that the payment of the bribe by the executives of the construction company was the "right" thing to do, given the situation.

ETHICAL ANALYSIS AND MORAL DILEMMAS

Multiple analysis just offers a useful means of rationalizing our intuitive beliefs, of justifying our almost automatic reactions, when we look at simple and obvious ethical issues such as foreign bribery. Multiple analysis, however, in my view provides close to an essential means of reaching a decision when we face a complex moral dilemma, where the economic performance and the social performance of our organization truly do seem to be in conflict. Does multiple analysis help us decide how much we owe to our employees, customers, suppliers, distributors, stockholders, and the general public, and does it help us to distinguish between those separate duties? I think that it does, and here I should like to use the moral problems encountered by former students—the ones that were described in the first chapter, on the nature of ethics in management—as illustrations. I don't believe that in these examples it will be possible to assume agreement between us—we all have our own moral standards, based upon our different ethical systems of belief—so I will not state my conclusions, just my methods of analysis:

Pricing of Checking Account Services

Small checking accounts were determined to be unprofitable for the bank, and consequently it was felt that a charge of $5.00 per month and $0.10 per transaction was warranted. The ethical problem was that the bank was in an urban area, with numerous older customers, many of them retired and living on Social Security, and the proposed charges would definitely diminish their standard of living. In short, the proposed changes would harm the older customers of the bank but improve the profits of the bank.

How can this situation be analyzed? Let us start by considering alternatives. Is it possible to design a new type of checking account, perhaps limited to a set number of transactions per month, that would be less expensive to administer? Is it possible to completely automate the transaction (checks and deposits) processing, to further reduce the costs? Assuming that neither is possible, then let us move along to economic analysis. What are the costs of maintaining the small accounts used by older people? How much would those costs increase, if the bank were the only one in the area not to make a monthly or transaction charge to retired customers, and consequently almost all of those people moved their accounts to this bank? What would the revenues be, if the charges were instituted? How many of the older customers would close their accounts, even though they are naturally afraid to hold all of their funds in cash in their homes and on their persons, and thus reduce our opportunity to achieve meaningful economies of scale?

Legal analysis is next. There is certainly no law against charging a fee for financial services, yet the bank could doubtless expect some protest by social and political organizations in the area that would voice an objection to charging a fee that fell primarily on low income, retired persons. The fee would contravene the presumed moral standards of a considerable segment of the population, and might eventually lead to legal restrictions.

Lastly, let us think about moral analysis. Universalism—everyone faced with a given situation should be forced to take the same action or make the same decision—does not seem too relevant here; I would be willing to have every banker faced with unprofitable accounts charge a fee for those accounts, were it not for the unfortunate consequences of that action in this instance. Utilitarianism, which deals with the consequences, does seem relevant here. The concept is often translated as "the greatest good for the greatest number", but those two combined concepts don't really help in moral analysis because the greatest number covers such a diversity of groups who often do not share equally in what is considered to be the greatest good. It is more useful in analyzing ethical dilemmas to think of utilitarianism as cost/benefit analysis, with the added step of considering who receives the benefits and who bears the costs. The benefits in this instance will go to the wealthier members of the community, as they are the large depositors who will receive the interest payments, or they are the stockholders of the bank who will receive the dividends, while the costs will be borne by the older and poorer people who have to pay the additional charges. That is troublesome. It certainly goes against the distributive justice concept that inequality in the distribution of benefits is legitimate, provided it in some way helps the less advantaged members of society. It also goes against the contributive liberty principle that our actions should increase, not decrease, the ability of all members of society to make their own decisions and lead their own lives.

How would I decide? I'm not certain—and I said earlier that I would not impose my views upon the reader—but at least I feel that I understand this situation much more fully, and would be better able to explain my decision to others much more rationally.

Delaying Shipments to Smaller Retailers

Small toy stores, bookstores, and clothing stores can survive against the competition of the "category killers"—the large specialty chains such as Toys-R-Us, Home Depot, Borders, and Burlington Coat Factory—only if they know the customers in a given market area well enough to be able to anticipate what those customers will want and then have that merchandise ready for their purchase when they want it. The problem, as expressed in Chapter 1, was that the manufacturers of popular merchandise do not fill orders in the sequence in which they are received. Instead, the manufacturers take care of their larger customers first, and ship to the national specialty chains—the category killers—before they begin to service the smaller, local stores.

Is that right? Economically I think that we all recognize the importance of economies of scale. Large national retailers are able to negotiate lower prices than small local shops for the merchandise they purchase because the costs of producing that merchandise in long runs and high volumes are so much less. But, this is not an issue of pricing. This is an issue of delaying shipments of popular merchandise to the small retailers so that the larger chains can be better served. This is an issue, apparently, of economic power rather than economic scale.

Are there alternatives? In this instance I would assume not. Some children's toys and clothing styles become very popular very quickly, and manufacturing capacity simply cannot be expanded quickly enough to fill all of the orders promptly. The question then becomes, "Which orders should be filled first?"

Economic analysis does not seem to help. It is understandable that manufacturers would wish to serve their largest customers first—even though the smaller ones may have ordered earlier—because of the economic power of those large customers, but that does not make such an action "right." Legally, there is no law that says orders have to be shipped in the sequence in which they have been received, even though I would assume that would be the moral standard of most members of the population.

Utilitarianism, which is the concept of the greatest good for the greatest number, does not seem to help much either. It is true that there are more small retailers than national chains, but there are more employees in the chains so the "greatest number" seems to be a wash. The final customers receive the same merchandise through either channel so the "greatest good" doesn't seem to be relevant either. Universalism, however, is very different. Do we want everyone who has scarce goods or services to supply—such as concert tickets, parking spaces, college admissions, or emergency room medical care—to allocate those goods and services on the basis of relative economic power? I assume that we do not. Most of us are low on any scale of relative economic power.

Distributive justice also seems to be helpful. Who are the least among us in this particular situation? I would think that they would be the owners of the small shops, who would have the least influence as compared to the much larger manufacturing companies and national chains, and therefore should not be harmed according to that principle. Contributive liberty is also relevant. Does the existing preferential treatment for the national chains help all of the rest of us work for our own self-development and self-fulfillment? It seems to me that such preferential treatment blocks the owners of the small shops from doing so, as well as the customers of those shops. Here once again I do not feel that I should burden you with the choice that I would make, but I do feel that I understand the situation much better, and would be able to explain my choice much more clearly.

Exaggerated or Misleading Claims in Advertising

The ethical problem in this instance is centered on advertising statements that were intended to deceive. "Up 87% over the past three years" was the heading on a mutual fund ad. This was true only over that specific time period. Over a longer time span the fund had not kept pace with the growth in the Dow-Jones averages. "8-1/2% interest" was the heading on a money market fund; there was a small asterisk, and down at the bottom of the page a footnote explained that the interest rate was for the first three months only. "Insured by (name of an insurance company)" was stated in every advertisement that mentioned customer accounts. The ads did not explain that the insurance company—which had an impressive sounding name such as Travelers Equitable Insurance Company of Wausau, Wisconsin even though it had no connection whatever with any of those firms—was a wholly owned and poorly financed subsidiary.

How do we analyze this situation? Start once again by looking at alternatives. Is it possible to develop an ad campaign that will be more effective and more truthful? I think that we can assume that the client—a financial services firm—was not irrevocably committed to being untruthful; they just wanted an advertising program that increased their annual revenues, and believed that deceptive statements would accomplish that purpose.

If the client does not wish to change the approach, then it is necessary to look at the economics of the ad campaign. What is the probable increase in revenues that can be directly attributed to the deceptive advertising, and how do these marginal revenues compare to the media costs? Most of us would like to believe that misleading slogans are not effective; that potential customers quickly "see through" that sort of untruth. Perhaps, however, we will find from market research that the ads are effective. They clearly are not illegal—or we would not see so many that are so similar in some sense—so we have to move to ethical analysis and moral reasoning.

Economic analysis assumes efficient markets, which means that customers should be fully informed about the properties of the product so that they can make informed choices. But, there is also a requirement that the customer take the time and make the effort to be fully informed—the old concept of "buyer beware"—so that economic analysis does not seem to really help in determining if these mildly deceptive ads are "wrong." Legal analysis does not seem to be helpful either. As stated above, there is no law against mildly deceptive advertising, doubtless because it is so hard to define exactly what is "mildly deceptive."

The philosophic doctrine of universalism does seems to be useful, however. The basic formulation of that doctrine would be, "Are you willing to agree that every person, wishing to increase his or her own self-advantage, should be free to make deliberately deceptive statements?" Let me explain, once again, that in using this first formulation of the Categorical Imperative it is important not to think of the consequences of the act, for that would bring in utilitarian concepts related to outcomes, and you would then not be building your ethical system of belief on a single principle. In this case, the single principle is your duty to other people to be consistent. You have to think about the type of world you want, and if you want a world in which judges don't try to deceive you, doctors don't try to deceive you, teachers don't try to deceive you, and friends don't try to deceive you, then you have to be consistent, and agree that advertisers should not try to do so either.

You could also look at the second formulation of the Categorical Imperative: that it is necessary to treat other people as ends in themselves, and not as means to our own ends, which means that we should consider the people reading the ads to be individuals worthy of dignity and respect, pursuing their own goals of happiness and self-improvement. The deliberate misleading of others does not seem to be treating them with dignity and respect, and it does not seem to be helping them to pursue their own goals of self-development and self-improvement. Instead, it seems to be treating them solely as means to the goal of the deceptive person, and denying them access to their individual objectives in life.

Working Conditions in a Manufacturing Plant

"The noise, the heat, the fumes, and the pace of work are close to intolerable" was the statement made to me, yet it was explained that funds would not be allocated to improve conditions without showing a substantial internal rate of return. Here, it would seem that economic analysis would be most meaningful. What are the costs in plant downtime, worker absence, and employee illness that bring low productivity and poor quality? How much could output and quality be improved, given better conditions? Economic theory insists that all costs be computed, including the personal costs of job safety and the social costs of environmental pollution; when this is done, remedial actions often do become economically rational.

Let us assume that this is an instance where improvements in the working conditions cannot be economically justified. Let us also assume that these working conditions are marginally lawful. What do we do then? Obviously, we are forced to use moral analysis, but moral analysis looking at alternatives, not just condemning the existing situation. Utilitarianism seems useful here. Who receives the benefits and who bears the costs of closing the plant? If we reduce the workforce or decrease the pay scale, in order to make the improvements economically justifiable, then who receives what benefits and who bears what costs? It is difficult to conceive of viable alternatives in depressed basic industries such as steel stampings and iron foundries, but it is important in moral analysis to go beyond simple "yes" or "no" choices. Professor Rawl's concept of social cooperation and distributive justice also seems relevant in looking at this situation. Which of these alternatives would most benefit the least advantaged among the members of the organization, who doubtless are the hourly paid employees? Would the increased cooperation then benefit the owners? It is at least worth considering that possibility in the search for a suitable alternative?

Large Expense Accounts for Senior Executives

The large expense accounts, which according to my informant included "family vacation tours, country club fees, and sporting event tickets" can be justified economically only if you conceive of a very competitive input labor market for senior executives and postulate a very short supply of those people with suitable talents. Then, it would be necessary to meet market prices, and if those market prices included untaxed payments of personal expenses, from a purely economic approach the payments would be justified. A second approach in economic analysis would be to conceive of a very competitive output product market for the company's goods and services, and propose that the "socializing opportunities" represented by the country club fees and sporting event tickets were needed to market those goods and services. Both would constitute a form of nonprice competition, on the absolute edge—if not over that edge—of acceptability within microeconomic theory.

Legally, the issue is even more questionable. Untaxed expense reimbursements are legal only if they represent true business costs rather than actual personal benefits. Customer entertaining on vacation trips and at country clubs and sporting events are certainly a common practice, and while they are not forbidden by any existing national laws, they are often banned by many internal company policies.

Do these hidden payments to senior executives create greater benefits for larger numbers of people associated with the company than any other possible use for the funds? I would assume not. Would we be willing to have every company make hidden—remember, these were classified as marketing expenses—payments to senior executives? Again, I would assume not. Do these hidden payments help the least among us? I would not believe so. Do they help others to reach their personal goals in life? I would not believe that either.

There is little to show that these hidden payments to senior executives are "right" and "just" and "fair" in any moral sense reflecting our duties and obligations to others. Yet, this is not a strong moral problem in that no one is being hurt all that badly by the practice, except for the owners of the firm who may or may not know of it. What should the ex-student who reported the incident to me do? That, of course, is up to her. It strikes me that there are clear career implications here for the practice seems to be firmly embedded in the culture of the organization. The issue for her is, "Where do I draw the line? When do I feel that the harm being caused to others is so 'wrong' that I must act, despite the potential damage to my own career?" That is the same issue faced by many ex-students in the first few years after graduation, and obviously it is an issue which they must decide for themselves. The intention of this book is to provide a guide for that decision.

Workforce Reductions

This is a strong moral problem in that the economic returns and the social obligations of the company are directly in conflict. It is also a common moral problem, given the recent increase in global competition and the current availability of low wage workers in many overseas areas.

My suggestion is that you start by looking at the alternatives to outright discharge, but unfortunately many of these alternatives are weak. Early retirement has a nice "voluntary" sound, but it is alleged not to be truly voluntary in many instances, and may leave people in an untenable position with a small pension and few marketable skills. Outplacement is another popular term, but it may be just a synonym for "we'll help you write your resume." The true problem is that, given the competitive nature of many basic industries, the number of alternatives for meaningful cost reduction is limited and reductions in personnel have to be considered.

Economic analysis is useful here. Exactly what will be the financial consequences of a smaller organization? Obviously, the overhead will be reduced, but will the competitive capability—in product development, market expansion, customer service, quality control, and worker productivity—improve? It is necessary for us to admit that some organizations have become so large, with so many layers of middle managers and so many groups of staff between the senior executives who can allocate resources and the operating personnel who can use them, that it is hard to improve competitive performance without middle management cutbacks. But, it is also necessary to admit that many workforce reductions impede rather than improve product development, market expansion, and customer service.

Moral analysis in workforce reductions has to focus on utilitarianism: who receives the benefits and who bears the costs, and is there any acceptable way to lessen those costs, or to redistribute those benefits? Here, the high managerial salaries and large expense accounts of the prior problem seem to be relevant. Would it be more equitable to spend somewhat more on the retraining of workers, the development of products, and the expansion of markets, and somewhat less on the salaries and bonuses of senior executives? Certainly the concepts of universal duty, distributive justice, and contributive liberty would tend to support an affirmative answer to that question.

Environmental Pollution

Pollution is a major problem faced by our society, with obvious consequences for individual health, recreational opportunities, and the quality of life for all. Why does the improper disposal of chemical wastes continue? It continues partially because of the uncertainty associated with improper disposal; it is hard for many people to realize that five gallons, or even fifty gallons, of a chemical used routinely in industry will be all that harmful when dumped in a landfill or a stream. And, in many instances they are correct: five gallons or even fifty gallons is not that harmful by itself; it is the aggregate of many five and fifty gallon amounts over a lengthy period of time that becomes exceedingly harmful.

In the illustration cited in the first chapter, a former student found that industrial solvents and degreasing solutions were being poured down a storm drain. I understand that, unfortunately, this is a common method of disposal. Economic analysis would reveal that the cost of proper disposal is often very high, which leads towards improper disposal, even though that clearly is an external cost which should be included in the calculations. Legal analysis would show that this improper disposal is certainly unlawful, but the law is difficult to enforce because of the problems of tracing the sources of pollution, whether the materials are poured into a public sewer or dumped onto a vacant lot. Ethical analysis seems to be equally definite. The greatest good for the greatest number would obviously require proper and safe combustion or burial, and few people would agree that all other firms, needing to dispose of used chemical compounds, should be free to just dump the material, secretly, into sewers or onto the landscape.

Property Tax Reductions

A major employer within a local community has substantial economic power, particularly if the employer has multiple plants in other locations, and consequently can move production, and employment, between those plants. This economic power is often used in pressing for tax concessions. In the illustration given in the first chapter, a company was pressing for a 50% tax reduction, just two years after they had received a 24% reduction. A large reduction of this nature would obviously impose tax increases or service reductions on the residents of the community.

Economic analysis would attempt to balance the benefits received by the community from the manufacturing plant, in the form of employment and tax payments, with the costs imposed on the community for the services needed by the plant and its employees. But the balance of benefits and costs is not all that matters in this instance. Here, we have to be concerned with the equitable receipt of those benefits and the equitable allocation of those costs; in short, is the system "fair" to everyone?

If we can establish, through legal analysis, that the tax assessment procedures were properly followed by the community, and that the tax rates are approximately equal for all classes or types of property, then the question we face is whether it is "proper" or "right" or "just" for residents who are not employed by the plant, and consequently receive none of the benefits, to be forced to pay part of the costs. This would seem to go against the precepts of universal duty, distributive justice, and contributive liberty. I promised not to state my opinions on these moral issues, but in this instance I will break that promise: The use of economic power to impose economic penalties on others who are much less able to influence events or to find other resources for their own self-development and self-fulfillments seems "wrong" to me.

Ethical Analysis and "Drawing the Line"

Ethical decisions of the nature that have been described above are not simple choices between right and wrong; they are complex judgments on the balance between the economic performance and the social performance of organizations. In all of the eight instances that were discussed—except perhaps for the reimbursements of personal recreational expenditures through the use of corporate expense accounts—the economic performance of the firm, measured by sales revenues, variable costs, fixed expenses or net profits, would be improved by the actions that were described. In all of the eight cases that were discussed the social performance of the firm, much more difficult to measure but expressed as some form of obligation to the managers, workers, customers, suppliers, distributors, and members of the local community, would be reduced. The questions, in each, became in summary, "What do we owe to our managers, our workers, our customers, our suppliers, our distributions, and our community? What do we owe to our owners?" How do we balance our economic performance and our social performance?

These are difficult questions to answer. They are difficult because of the essential conflict between the two dissimilar quantities: economic performance and social performance. They are also difficult because each question has numerous alternative solutions—these are not simple "yes" or "no" choices—and the consequences of the alternatives extend through- out society, with outcomes in which the benefits and costs are often mixed, and the probabilities of those outcomes are frequently uncertain. How do we decide when faced with moral problems of this complexity? Multi- ple analysis—using economic, legal, and moral forms of reasoning— appears—to me at all events—to make the issues much clearer, and the "right" or "proper" or "just" decision more apparent.

Unfortunately, reaching the "right" or "proper" or "just" answer often is not enough. It is also necessary to decide when you will insist that your view of what is "right" and "proper" and "just" be recognized, and then implemented by the organization. One option is to explain your concerns to people, and gain some converts. Another option is to explain your analysis, and gain some more. But it is seldom possible to achieve unanimity in an ethical issue because each individual's moral standards, value judgments, and career ambitions are so personal, and so deeply held. Managers will often compromise on marketing and production and financial problems; they often will not even acknowl- edge major ethical issues.

What do you do when you feel strongly about an ethical problem— a conflict between the economic performance and the social perfor- mance of your firm—and you find that no compromise or even acknowledgement is possible? Do you walk away from the problem, or do you take some action? Where do you draw the line?

Firstly, it is necessary to recognize that people can legitimately differ in their views of what should be done to resolve a moral dilemma. A refusal to compromise—or even to acknowledge—does not automatically mean that others in the organization are "wrong." People can differ in their views of moral problems because the relative weighting they place on the economic, legal, and ethical forms of analysis may vary. People may differ because the ethical systems upon which their standards for moral reasoning are based can vary. And, it is also necessary to recog- nize that people can differ in their views of what constitutes an ethical dilemma. Some people are much less concerned with social performance, and much more concerned with economic performance, than others. What do you do under those circumstances, if you find a situation or an issue you believe to be deeply wrong according to your personal moral standards, yet you recognize that you are in the minority within your portion of the organization?

Let us assume that you are not the president or a senior executive of your company, able to take whatever action you believe to be "just." Let us also assume that there is no ombudsman—generally an older and respected member of the organization who has been relieved of direct responsibility for management, and has been designated to counsel privately with other employees on personal problems and ethical issues—within the firm. Let us lastly assume that you have looked for alternatives, and found none, and have tried to explain your concerns to your immediate superior, and been rejected. What do you do? What do you do if you have found large amounts of toxic wastes being stored in leaking 55 gallon drums and been told, "Forget it; it's none of your business." What do you do if you have found that employees are being subjected to unsafe working conditions, and been told, "We don't have the money to fix it." What do you do if you find that payments are being made to senior executives for nonbusiness related expenses, and been told, "Keep quiet about this; it goes on all the time." Where do you draw the line, between what you will accept, and what you will not accept?

This is the most fundamental moral issue in management, for it places a person's career in jeopardy. How do you decide if the resolution of the moral dilemma you have encountered is worth your career? I think that it necessary to use only the most basic moral reasoning:

Economic. Does this action produce more wanted outputs, or use less scarce inputs than any other alternative; that is, is it efficient?

Legal. Does this action meet the assumed minimal moral standards of a majority of our fellow citizens; that is, does it follow the law?

Beneficiency. Who is going to be benefited, and how much, and who is going to be hurt, and how badly?

Consistency. Could I permit everyone to take this same action, or an action closely similar to this, in which I would be the person to be hurt?

Justice. Will the least advantaged among us be treated the worst, for they are the ones least able to influence events and must consequently be protected?

Liberty. Will this reduce the opportunities of all of us for free, informed choice relative to our own self-development and self-fulfillment?

In the next chapter we will look at changes in the structure and systems of an organization that can more readily resolve the ethical conflicts between economic and social performance, and more easily avoid the necessity for an individual to make the fundamental moral choice between his or her career and his or her responsibility.

CASE 5–1

Conflict of Duties in Accounting and Finance

The managers of a business firm obviously have duties to their stockholders who are the owners of the company and benefited by its profits. The managers also have duties to their stakeholders who are the people associated with the company in some way and affected by its actions. These two sets of duties frequently come into conflict. One of the basic moral responsibilities of management is to resolve those conflicts in ways that can be considered to be "right" and "just" and "fair." How would you resolve the following three conflicts in the functional areas of accounting and finance; all of these actions were legal at the time they were proposed or considered:

1. *Reorganizing a company to reduce unemployment costs.* In the southeastern United States during the late 1980s many of the companies in the petroleum and construction industries were forced to substantially reduce employment as a lengthy business decline caused by inexpensive oil imports hit the region. The discharged workers collected unemployment benefits from the states, of course, but the reserves for those benefits were soon exhausted. The state of Texas passed a law to raise the unemployment compensation tax to replenish the reserves. The amount of the additional tax to be paid by each company was to be proportional to the number of workers that had been laid off by that company over the past five years. Large firms that had laid off large numbers of workers found that it would be far less expensive to reorganize their operations, combine their divisions, and form a totally new company. The new company, which could be chartered for less than $100,000 in legal and accounting fees, would of course have no prior history of laying off workers, and would therefore be exempt from the additional tax. For some large firms which had laid off hundreds or even thousands of workers in the past, the savings from a new charter would be in range of $250,000 to $2,500,000 per year. Is it "right" for these large firms to reorganize operations, combine divisions, and charter a new company to lower their unemployment compensation costs? What do the senior executives in a company "owe" to other citizens in the state in which it is located? What do the accountants and attorneys "owe" to those citizens?

2. *Using nonverbal language to convey inside information.* During the period of unfriendly take-overs and forced acquisitions in the late 1980s many brokerage firms formed risk arbitrage departments to

invest in the stocks of companies that were considered "in play." The profits were immense if a brokerage firm could buy stock in a company during the "run up" before the final price was set and announced. The risks, however, were equally great because many of the acquisitions that were widely talked about and largely expected never took place. Access to reliable information was the key, but the investment bankers, lawyers, and accountants who were involved in the take-over and acquisition process were forbidden by law to discuss any details of their activities with persons outside that process. Robert Freeman, at that time the head of risk arbitrage at Goldman, Sachs & Company and a well known, wealthy figure on Wall Street, took the approach of calling the principal investment banker involved in a proposed take-over to discuss recently publicized information as the process neared completion. He said that he could tell by the "anxious tone of voice"[1] whenever there was likely to be a problem. The U.S. Attorney's Office attempted to arrest Mr. Freeman for the use of this "anxious tone" as inside information. Government officials pointed out that few other arbitrageurs and no small investors would have been able to reach these investment bankers by telephone, let alone know them well enough to judge their outlook by their tone of voice or, as the government alleged, by the very brief and enigmatic tips that were exchanged. One attorney for Mr. Freeman admitted that Mr. Freeman's wide range of friendships did give him an advantage, but said that was immaterial. "The market is not and never has been a level playing field," he explained.[2] Another attorney for Mr. Freeman said that the government would have to define insider trading much more clearly before indicting his client. "A legitimate business man is entitled to know what the rules of the game are before he gets carted off to jail," he claimed.[3] Is it "right" for Mr. Freeman to obtain market information through professional friendships and personal telephone calls? What, if anything, does a brokerage firm executive "owe" to other investors in the financial markets?

3. *Changing transfer prices and overhead costs to reduce taxes.* It is well known that many foreign companies that operate in the United States pay substantially less in corporate income taxes than American firms in exactly the same industry with approximately the same cost structure. The reason is that the foreign countries in which these companies are based usually have corporate income tax rates that are much lower than those in the U.S., and consequently it is in the self-interests of the foreign companies to recognize their profits at home. This can be done by changing the transfer prices at which their products are moved from one country to another, and by allocating the shared costs of their overhead budgets more to one country than another. It is not so well known that globalized American companies often do exactly the same thing, but in reverse. An American company with manufacturing and marketing operations throughout the world can arrange to recognize their profits

abroad. Is it "right" for globalized American companies to reduce their tax liabilities by recognizing their profits in foreign countries? What do the managers of large American companies "owe" to the other citizens of their country?

Class Assignment. Decide what you believe is "owed" to each group of stakeholders in this series of problems.

Footnotes

1. *The New York Times,* August 28, 1989, p.22.
2. Ibid.
3. Ibid.

CASE 5–2

George Kacmarek

George Kacmarek was a graduate of the BBA program at the University of Michigan. He went to work for one of the large auto supply firms in Detroit that produced stamped metal parts for the car companies. The following is an almost verbatim account of a moral problem he encountered during his first week on the job.

On the 2nd or 3rd day at work I was sent from the office out to the plant to pick up some requisition slips from the foreman in one of the tool rooms. I don't know if you have ever been in a big stamping plant, but they are noisy and confusing. They have these big presses going up and coming down, and you can't hear yourself think. In our plant they have more than 100 presses, all under one roof, but with paint booths, tool cribs, loading docks, and storage bins scattered all around. I got lost.

I didn't want to admit that I was lost, so I couldn't ask any of the workers for directions. They probably couldn't hear me anyway. I went into what I thought would be an office where I could ask for directions, but it was a record storage area, with row after row of steel shelving reaching close to the ceiling, loaded with thousands of cardboard files, each marked by a number. There was a door at one end, and I was heading in that direction when I heard the voice of the plant manager talking to another person. The plant manager was from New York City, and had an accent that you could remember very easily. I had only met him once, but I recognized his voice right away.

The plant manager said, "I want $5,000 this time. That's a nice round figure, and it will help me to remember (name of a large steel supply firm) for the rest of the year."

The other person said, "George, you're getting greedy. You've given us good business, and we appreciate it, but it's not worth five bills."

The plant manager got upset and told the man, "Look, you'll be out on your fat rear end if I say the word. We'll start running quality checks on your stuff until we find some that won't meet specs, and then we'll reject everything you've sent us for a month."

This didn't faze the other guy at all; he said, "George, we know the score. You don't have to tell us. But we can't go $5,000. We'll go $3,000 now, and $3,000 at the end of the year if everything stays smooth and if your volume holds up, but that's the best that we can do."

The plant manager grumbled about that but eventually he agreed to it, and both men went out the door at the end without seeing me. I went out the other door as fast as I could, and wandered around on the shop floor for awhile. I didn't know what to do.

Class Assignment.   What would you do in this situation? Make a set of specific recommendations for George Kacmarek.

CASE 5–3

Hydro-Quebec and the Great Whale Controversy

Hydro-Quebec is the government owned public utility in the Canadian province of Quebec. It supplies 98% of the electrical energy used in that province. Most of the energy is produced in the northern reaches of the province, by means of hydroelectric dams and generators. Hydroelectric power, of course, is an almost ideal form of energy; there are no fuel costs, no toxic residues, and no harmful emissions. It is, in essence, an indirect form of solar power.

Northern Quebec is also an almost ideal location for the generation of hydro-electric power. The province contains nearly 10% of all the fresh water on earth. Climatic conditions bring large amounts of rainfall, snowfall, and thick, dense fog. Geological conditions feature a rocky substructure that keeps most of the water on the surface, and low mountains with a constant slope towards Hudson's Bay that funnel it into rapidly flowing streams and rivers. The rivers, many with steep rocky sides, can easily be dammed.

Dams, and the impounded bodies of water behind each dam, take a lot of land, and the land of Northern Quebec, while ideal for the hydro-electric generation of power, is not vacant. It has been inhabited for centuries by Cree Indians and Inuit Eskimos, both of whom live by fishing, hunting, and trapping along the streams, rivers, and lakes of the region. For years they have objected to any attempt to utilize the resources of the region, including the electric power potential.

By the mid-1970s, however, the traditional patterns of tribal life had changed for both peoples, and the Cree and the Inuit were caught halfway between the old and the new. They were increasingly dependent upon modern equipment such as snowmobiles, outboard motors, hunting rifles, and the manufactured clothing and housing that turned out to be much warmer and more convenient than the traditional materials and methods, yet their hunting, fishing, and trapping lifestyle did not generate the cash income necessary to pay for these products. Trapping, which long had been the economic mainstay of Cree and Inuit communities, declined rapidly in importance in the years following 1960 as a result of the refusal by many Western European and North American women to wear fur coats, part of a growing environmental protection and animal rights movement. The price received by native hunters for a beaver pelt, trapped along the rivers and streams of Northern Quebec, fell from $70.00 to $12.00 during the period 1960 to 1975.

In 1975 an agreement was reached with the leaders of the Cree and Inuit peoples to build dams and construct power stations upon a limited portion of the northern land mass of Quebec. This agreement, known formally as the James Bay and Northern Quebec Territorial Agreement, was signed by representatives of the Federal Government (Ottawa), the Provincial Government (Quebec), the utility (Hydro-Quebec) and the native peoples (both Cree and Inuit).

The agreement included a one-time payment of $550 million that was to be used for improved education, housing, health care, and local development. The effects of this payment can be seen today in such villages as Whapmagoostui on the southern edge of the sub-Arctic wilderness. Two new schools were constructed and staffed, along with a new community center, a new airport, a new hockey rink, a new medical clinic, a new supermarket and department store, and new housing. Children from the village had always been eligible for national college scholarships, but now for the first time they were able to take advantage of that opportunity. With a college education and graduate study in law and medicine came a much greater integration into the economic life of the province, though that integration required movement away from the northern territories. The college graduates, however, frequently sent money home for the support of their relatives. The improved conditions from all causes were acknowledged by the leaders of the Cree community:

There's no doubt we are living a lot better now. (Statement of Robbie Dick, Chief of the Whapmagoostui Cree, quoted in Gannet News Service, Nov. 22nd, 1991)

The same results could be seen throughout the entire northern region by 1990. Improved housing and health care brought a substantial increase in the native population. Infant mortality decreased by 50%. The average life span increased by 30%. The total number of Cree Indians went from 6,300 in 1975 to 11,500 in 1990. The base population of the Inuit Eskimos had never been accurately counted, but it was felt that the same percentage increase occurred there also.

(Before the agreement) the Cree communities were collections of shacks and tents around trading stores. My people lived on the land six to eight months of the year, and came together only during the summers. The summer shacks were crowded, tuberculosis was common, and increasingly the sick and the invalid had to stay at the trading posts throughout the year, living off welfare. All that has changed. (Statement of Matthew Coon-Come, Grand Chief of the Cree, quoted in Gannett News Service, Nov. 22nd, 1991).

It's for the better, only for the better. (Statement of Anthony Ittoshak, Chief of the Kuujjarapik Inuit, quoted in "A Question of Power," videotape produced by the University of Michigan. Note: "Kuujjarapik," translated into English, means "Great Whale").

The James Bay and Northern Quebec Territorial Agreement of 1975 divided the land in northern Quebec, a total of slightly over 411,000 square miles, into three major categories. These categories are important because they were part of an effort to isolate the native villages from the harmful impacts of the hydroelectric construction and operation:

Category I—5,145 square miles with no hydroelectric development permitted. This area was reserved for the existing villages. It constituted an area the size of Rhode Island and Connecticut combined, and surrounded each of the native communities with a substantial buffer zone. No village was to be moved, except for one in which the inhabitants asked to be relocated, closer to James Bay. No hydroelectric projects whatsoever were to be permitted here, except for power transmission lines to the villages.

Category II—62,678 square miles with some development permitted. This area, the size of New Hampshire, Vermont, and New York State combined, was divided into large plots adjacent to each of the native villages in Category I, and these plots were reserved for the exclusive hunting, fishing and trapping needs of the native peoples. No hydroelectric projects that would change the character of the land, or its suitability for hunting, fishing, and trapping, were to be permitted here.

Category III—343,521 square miles in which the hydroelectric development was to be concentrated. Not all of this land was to be developed; in fact, the dams and impounded lakes behind each dam were expected to cover less than 2% of the total category area. But, it was acknowledged that the dams and lakes would change the character of the land, and its accessibility for hunting, fishing, and trapping. It would be hard, for example, for native hunters to cross some of the larger impounded bodies of water that might be 25 miles wide and 100 or more miles long.

Construction started in 1975 in the southern portions of the region covered by the James Bay and Northern Quebec Territorial Agreement. This construction was to be in four phases, and by 1992 the situation for each phase was as follows:

LaGrande I	Fully completed in 1985	10,400 MW
LaGrande II	Expected completion in 1995	4,500 MW
Great Whale	Planning started in 1991	3,100 MW
Nottaway	Planning to start in 1998	8,400 MW
Far North	Not under consideration	23,000 MW
Total		49,400 MW

"MW" stands for megawatts. Each megawatt equals one million watts of electric power. A more understandable translation is that 1,000 MW is the output of a single modern coal-fired or nuclear generating plant. The total potential of the region, then, was the equivalent of nearly 50 modern generating plants.

Planning for the Great Whale project (named for the principal river in that region) had started in 1991, but had been held up by important legal questions throughout 1992 and 1993. Representatives of the Cree Indians and Inuit Eskimos said that they had given permission for the two LaGrande river projects, which emptied into James Bay, but not for the Great Whale and Nottaway river projects, which emptied into Hudson's Bay much further to the north. They also said they had not realized the scale of the development nor the impact of the development upon their lives when they signed the James Bay and Northern Quebec Territorial Agreement in 1975.

> Flooding 5,000 square kilometers does not sound like much, but when you see it, and what once was a river is now a sea, it really hits you. (Statement of Albert Diamond, Member of the Grand Council of the Cree, quoted in the "Question of Power" videotape produced by the University of Michigan)

The James Bay and Northern Quebec Territorial Agreement is a 31 chapter, 450 page legal document; it is certainly understandable that different interpretations of some of the provisions in that lengthy and detailed a pact could easily occur. The Cree Indians and Inuit Eskimos were represented by attorneys sympathetic to their cause, but it is also understandable that many of the native peoples did not fully recognize the huge size of the dams, reservoirs, and power stations that were to be built upon their lands and impact their lives. And, the leaders now say with some anger, neither the attorneys nor themselves were forewarned at all about one of the major environmental impacts of the project: the release of methyl mercury into the food chain.

Reservoirs flooding low scrub forests such as those in northern Quebec have been found to leach mercury from the decaying vegetation, and transform it into methyl mercury which enters the food chain and is concentrated in certain species of fish. The mercury levels in non-predatory fish such as whitefish which live by eating small organisms and insects stay within the U.S. Environmental Protection Agency's safe guidelines. Mercury levels in predatory fish such as trout, pike, and walleye which live by eating other fish come considerably above those guidelines. Engineers at Hydro-Quebec say that they could not have anticipated these results, which apparently occur only in northern reservoirs under very specific conditions. Representatives of the Cree and Inuit say that whether or not the mercury contamination could have been anticipated is beside the point; they say that they should not now have the major fish species in their area further contaminated. They want the development stopped.

The present situation is that, as a result of the suit brought by the Cree Indians and Inuit Eskimos questioning a very basic interpretation of the James Bay and Northern Quebec Territorial Agreement and alleging unforeseen mercury contamination along with other adverse impacts, a Dominion Court in Ottawa has ordered the Quebec Government to do a binding review of the social, economic, and environmental impact of the Great Whale project. The Dominion Court also ordered Hydro-Quebec to pay $5 million to the native peoples to enable them to fully participate in the review process, and to hire consultants and attorneys to represent their side.

The native peoples also brought the dispute to the United States, where New York, New Hampshire, and Vermont had agreed to purchase approximately 20% of the power from the total project, when completed. The purchase of the hydroelectric power from Northern Quebec had appealed to officials in New England and New York because the power was "clean" with few air pollution or water pollution problems, and because it eliminated any disputes over "sitting" new plants within their own region. No one wants a large conventional power plant, with the heavy rail traffic required for input fuel and unsightly high-tension towers needed for output distribution, in the backyard of their home or business.

The sale of power from the project also appealed to officials in Quebec. Prices for power are almost twice as high in New England and New York as in Canada, due to the lack of fuel costs for hydro-generation in Canada. The profits from the sale were expected to come to well over a billion dollars a year, which—as Hydro-Quebec was owned by the province—was expected to be used to improve primary and secondary education throughout Quebec.

The Cree Indians, in a public relations coup, paddled down the Hudson River in native boats and dress, appearing on the television news each evening, asking viewers not to buy the power that would destroy their land and their culture. Governor Cuomo of New York canceled his state's contract to purchase power, saying additional electricity was not needed for the foreseeable future, and public utility executives in Vermont and New Hampshire wavered also, but the approaching deregulation of electrical utilities in the U.S. opened up many other markets for the Canadian power. Under deregulation, utilities will no longer enjoy exclusive service territories with rates set by the state governments. Instead, utilities will be permitted to serve customers regardless of their location, and will be forced to compete for those customers on price. The low cost hydropower from Quebec, obviously, becomes extremely attractive under those conditions.

There is no question but that hydroelectric power is cheaper to produce than other forms of electrical energy:

$0.042/kilowatt hour for hydroelectric

$0.062/kilowatt hour for nuclear

$0.078/kilowatt hour for thermal (coal, oil, or natural gas)

Co-generation, which involves use of the remaining heat from a coal, oil, or natural gas fired plant for industrial purposes after the energy has been extracted, provides additional income that can—in essence—cut the cost of thermal energy back to $0.073/kilowatt hour, but that figure is still far above the nonfuel costs of hydro.

The province of Quebec has used their supply of low cost electrical energy from the north as a comparative advantage in their effort to spur industrial development in the south, much as many of the countries in Southeast Asia have used their supply of low cost labor for the same purpose. Quebec until recently was a rural province, dependent upon agriculture and forestry, with high unemployment and extensive poverty. Most visitors see only the cosmopolitan areas surrounding Montreal and Quebec City; they do not encounter the much poorer conditions in the interior. Energy dependent industries such as aluminum and magnesium smelting, and iron and steel recycling, have been encouraged to start on the banks of the St. Lawrence River which, of course, provides sea access to global markets.

The province of Quebec has also used their supply of low cost electrical energy for such domestic purposes as home heating, which has lessened their dependence upon foreign oil and their need to make foreign payments. The province is attempting to encourage the use of electric cars, for exactly the same two purposes.

Lastly, the province of Quebec has stressed the pollution-free nature of their low cost electrical energy. A coal fired 1,000 MW generating plant, even with all of the modern pollution control technology installed and operating, will still produce 1,600,000 tons of carbon dioxide per year (the cause of global warming) and 30,000 tons of sulfur dioxide per year (the cause of acid rain). Hydroelectric generation produces none of these gases and, unlike nuclear energy, has no toxic wastes that need disposal.

The leaders of the Cree and Inuit peoples say that they recognize the many economic, social, and environmental advantages of the hydroelectric power, both for others and for themselves, but they believe strongly that it is wrong to force the generation projects onto their land, to the detriment of their culture:

> It's very hard to explain to white people what we mean when we say our land is part of our life. We're like rocks and trees, beaver and caribou. We belong here. We will not leave. (Statement of Robbie Dick, chief of the Whapmagoostui Cree, quoted in the *New York Times,* Oct. 29th, 1990)

> It's always us who are asked to pay. We're the ones who are asked to give up our water, to give up our trees. We're the ones who are told, "Move over children." (Statement of Matthew Coon Come, Grand Chief of the Cree, quoted in the *Toronto Star,* Feb. 2nd, 1992)

Class Assignment.   What should be done relative to the Great Whale project and to the other projects further north in Quebec that have the potential to produce such large amounts of clean, inexpensive electrical energy? It is suggested that you start by listing all of the benefits and all of the harms. Then decide. What would you do? If you wish to delay the decision, to see if new technologies such as solar or wind power might become available, at least consider who will be hurt and how badly by that delay if a shortage of electrical power should develop. What would life in an urban society be like if there were a serious shortage? All large scale decisions harm someone, including the decision to do nothing. Recognize the full extent of those harms in your decision.

CHAPTER 6

Managerial Ethics and Organizational Design

We are concerned in this book with ethical dilemmas: decisions and actions faced by managers in which the economic performance and the social performance of the organization are in conflict. These are situations in which someone to whom the organization has some form of obligation—employees, customers, suppliers, distributors, stockholders, or the general population in the area where the company operates—is going to be hurt or harmed in some way, while the company is going to profit. The question is how to decide: how to find a balance between economic performance and social performance that a manager can say with some degree of certainty is "right" and "proper" and "just."

In the last chapter it was suggested that it is necessary for a manager facing an ethical dilemma to use multiple forms of analysis, to make use of economic concepts, legal precepts, and philosophical principles in sequence to find that balance. After all, if a manager's decision or action follows impersonal market forces, conforms to published legal requirements, provides substantial benefits to large numbers of people, is an action we can wish that everyone would take when faced with the same set of decision alternatives and background factors, is "fair" in the sense of increasing the willingness of others to work towards greater social cooperation, and is "open" in the sense of expanding the ability of others to choose for themselves, then perhaps we can say with some degree of certainty that that decision is "right" and "proper" and "just."

So far, however, we have thought of the managers facing these ethical dilemmas in which the social performance and the economic performance of their firms are in obvious conflict as being free individuals, isolated from organizational influences, able to choose the "right" and "proper" and "just" as they see the "right" and "proper" and "just." That may not be an accurate view. There may be explicit organizational pressures that affect that choice. These organizational pressures may tend to push the decision away from the social performance and towards the economic performance of the firm. These organizational pressures may be so extreme that they force the manager to make the fundamental moral choice between his or her personal career and his or her social responsibility.

Let us look at some of these fundamental moral choices and explicit organizational pressures, and let us use as an example one of the most damaging industrial accidents of the past decade: the wreck of the Exxon Valdez.

THE WRECK OF THE EXXON VALDEZ

At 9:30 P.M. on Thursday, the 23rd of March 1989, the oil tanker Exxon Valdez left the oil terminal at Valdez, Alaska loaded with 1.26 million barrels of crude petroleum from the North Slope producing fields. The Valdez is the largest tanker owned by Exxon. It is nearly 1,000 feet long and weighs, fully loaded, 280,000 tons.

When the ship left port, it was under the command of Captain William Murphy, the harbor pilot. Harbor pilots are responsible for steering both incoming and outgoing tankers through the Valdez Narrows, a 1/2 mile wide approach to the port at Valdez. After exiting the Narrows and achieving the sea lanes in Prince William Sound, Captain Murphy turned over command to Captain Joseph Hazelwood and left the ship. Captain Murphy testified later that he had smelled alcohol on the breath of Captain Hazelwood, but that he had made no comment and had taken no action. He knew that it was common practice for both the officers and crew of oil tankers to drink while in port. (See Exhibit 6–1.)

Captain Hazelwood, immediately after assuming command, radioed the Coast Guard and requested permission to alter course to avoid large chunks of ice that had broken loose from the Columbia Glacier and were floating in the outbound shipping lane. The permission was granted. Captain Hazelwood then turned over command of the vessel to the Third Mate, Mr. Gregory Cousins, and went below to his cabin. Mr. Cousins was not licensed to pilot a ship in the sea channels approaching Valdez. Mr. Cousins and others later testified that it was common practice to turn over command of oil tankers to non-licensed officers.

Captain Hazelwood had set the automatic pilot to steer the ship southward into the inbound shipping lane, and he had instructed Mr. Cousins to maintain that course until after the ice chunks from the glaciers were past, and then to return northward to the outbound lane. No inbound traffic was expected, and permission for this course change had been granted by the Coast Guard, so no danger was anticipated. At 11:55 Mr. Cousins ordered a course change of 10 degree right rudder to bring the tanker back to the proper lane within the channel. There was no response. At 12:04 the lookout, who was on the bridge rather than at the normal station on the bow of the tanker, sighted the lighted buoy marking Bligh

EXHIBIT 6–1

Diagram of the Approaches to Valdez Harbor, and Listing of the Events that Led to the Accident on March 24, 1989

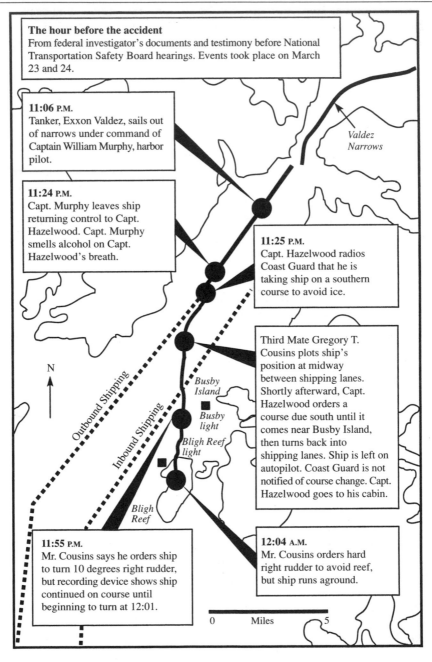

The hour before the accident
From federal investigator's documents and testimony before National Transportation Safety Board hearings. Events took place on March 23 and 24.

11:06 P.M.
Tanker, Exxon Valdez, sails out of narrows under command of Captain William Murphy, harbor pilot.

Valdez Narrows

11:24 P.M.
Capt. Murphy leaves ship returning control to Capt. Hazelwood. Capt. Murphy smells alcohol on Capt. Hazelwood's breath.

11:25 P.M.
Capt. Hazelwood radios Coast Guard that he is taking ship on a southern course to avoid ice.

Third Mate Gregory T. Cousins plots ship's position at midway between shipping lanes. Shortly afterward, Capt. Hazelwood orders a course due south until it comes near Busby Island, then turns back into shipping lanes. Ship is left on autopilot. Coast Guard is not notified of course change. Capt. Hazelwood goes to his cabin.

N

Outbound Shipping

Inbound Shipping

Busby Island

Busby light

Bligh Reef light

Bligh Reef

11:55 P.M.
Mr. Cousins says he orders ship to turn 10 degrees right rudder, but recording device shows ship continued on course until beginning to turn at 12:01.

12:04 A.M.
Mr. Cousins orders hard right rudder to avoid reef, but ship runs aground.

0   Miles   5

SOURCE: *New York Times,* May 22, 1989, p.10

Reef, a rock outcropping only 13 to 40 feet beneath the surface. Mr. Cousins ordered emergency hard right rudder. Again, there was no response. In the hearings that followed the accident, it was determined that either Captain Hazelwood had not informed Mr. Cousins that he had placed the ship on automatic pilot, or that Mr. Cousins and the helmsman had not remembered to disconnect the automatic pilot, which prevented manual steering of the vessel.

At 12:05 A.M. the Exxon Valdez ran aground on Bligh Reef. The hull was punctured in numerous places; 260,000 barrels, approximately 11,000,000 gallons of crude oil, began to spill from the badly ruptured tanks. It would eventually be the largest oil spill in the history of the North American petroleum industry. It would eventually cause immense harm, estimated in the billions of dollars, to the livelihood of the people living within the area, and immense damage, which can't be estimated in dollar terms, to the quality of the Alaskan environment.

At 12:28 A.M. one of the officers on the ship radioed to the Coast Guard that it was aground on Bligh Reef. "Are you leaking oil?" a Coast Guard operator asked. "I think so," was the reply.[1]

At 3:23 A.M. members of the Coast Guard boarded the Exxon Valdez, and reported that oil was gushing from the tanker. "We've got a serious problem," radioed the Coast Guard officer on board the tanker. "There's nobody here.... Where's Alyeska?"[2]

AFTERMATH OF THE WRECK

"Alyeska" was the Alyeska Pipeline Service Company which both managed the oil pipeline which brought crude oil 800 miles from the oil fields at Prudhoe Bay to Valdez, and ran the oil terminal at Valdez. It was responsible through a formal agreement with the state of Alaska for the containment and recovery of all oil spills within the harbor and sea lanes leading towards Valdez. That agreement was expressed in a detailed written plan, 250 pages long, that listed the equipment and personnel that were to be kept available by Alyeska, and the actions that were to be taken by Alyeska, to react promptly to oil spills. The stated goal of the plan was to encircle any serious oil spill with floating containment booms within five hours of the first report of the occurrence, and to recover 50% of the spill within 48 hours. The stated goal was well known within the area, and accounted for the perplexity of the Coast Guard officer. When he reported, "There's nobody here," he was referring not to the captain and crew of the tanker, but to the oil spill recovery team and equipment from Alyeska.

At 6:00 A.M. on Friday the 24th of March (6 hours after the accident), officials from Exxon flew over the grounded tanker for the first time, and reported a massive oil slick streaming away from the tanker. They contacted the Alyeska oil terminal, and ordered a quicker response and greater effort from the personnel at the terminal. The problem, the manager at the terminal reported, was that the single barge capable of handling the long containment booms had been out of service for nine weeks, and had been unloaded for repairs. They could still use the barge, despite the lack of repair, but the single employee who was capable of operating the crane needed for reloading had not yet reported for work. When that employee was contacted (it was his day off) and did report, it was found that only about half of the containment booms that were listed in the emergency plan and should have been readily available were actually in stock. By 2:30 P.M. the barge was loaded and had departed for the wreck site, carrying all of the containment booms that were available, and a number of centrifugal pumps to help in removing the remaining oil from the Valdez. None of the 10" diameter hoses, which would be needed to connect the pumps and transfer the oil, could be found among the emergency supplies; it was necessary to fly lengths of the huge hoses from Seattle to Valdez. The transfer of the remaining oil in the Valdez was delayed until those hoses arrived.

At 7:36 A.M. on Saturday the 25th of March (31-1/2 hours after the accident), Exxon began pumping oil from the Valdez to a second tanker moored alongside, the Baton Rouge. At about the same time, seven Alyeska "skimmers," or boats with vacuum equipment designed to siphon oil off the surface of the water, arrived at the site. The skimmers, however, were designed to recover oil that had been bunched in a compact mass by the containment booms. Those booms were still not in place, due to a shortage of tugs and some degree of confusion in the means of unloading the heavy booms, connecting them, and placing them in the sea. By nightfall, only 1,200 barrels of oil had been recovered by the skimmers.

At 11:00 A.M. on Sunday, the 26th of March (59 hours after the accident), the Exxon Valdez was finally encircled by containment booms. It had taken 2-1/2 days to set the booms in place, despite the original plan which called for full containment of any spill within five hours. Because of the shortage of booms, most of the oil was outside the containment area, in a slick that now covered 12 square miles. The wave action had begun to convert the crude oil to an emulsified "mousse" mixture of oil and water that quadrupled the volume. This emulsified mixture now lay 5" to 9" thick upon the surface of the sea, and winds were spreading that mixture throughout Prince William Sound. It had begun to swathe the islands and beaches with solid black bands of petroleum "gunk," the accepted term for the residue that is left after the more volatile elements in crude oil have evaporated. Eventually the mousse mixture would stretch 700 miles along the Alaskan coastline, spoiling fishery resources, wildlife refuges, and national parks in one of the most scenic regions of the world, and killing birds, fish, and mammals in one of the prime marine habitats of the world.

CAUSES OF THE WRECK

At one level of analysis the causes of this accident can be considered to be simple and obvious: an intoxicated captain set the wrong course, and the tanker ran aground on the most clearly chartered reef in Prince William Sound, 10 miles south of the proper shipping channel. It is necessary to remember, however, that intoxication has never been proven. Captain Hazelwood admitted that he had been drinking prior to sailing, but he has maintained that he was not drunk, and no witnesses could be found to swear that he was drunk, at the time of the accident. And, it is also necessary to admit that there were numerous other factors *under the control of the company* that contributed both to the grounding of the tanker, and to the slowness of the response to the spill.

In this discussion of the accident and the consequences of that accident, I should like to limit the causes to those that could have been corrected by the Exxon Corporation. There was an obvious lack of attention by the Coast Guard, which should have been able to monitor and correct the course of the tanker on their radar, and there was an obvious lack of supervision by the state regulators, who should have insisted that Alyeska Pipeline Service Company be prepared to follow the written agreement on the containment and recovery of oil spills. But, in this chapter we are looking at the influence of organizational pressures on the moral decisions of managers, and so I wish to exclude the federal and state agencies. Despite that exclusion in this account, I think that most impartial observers would agree that both the U.S. Coast Guard and the Alaskan Department of Natural Resources bear some of the blame for the occurrence and the severity of the accident.

What were the factors under the control of the Exxon Corporation that led firstly to the occurrence and then to the severity of the accident? Let me suggest that they can be divided into three different levels of causation that correspond roughly with three different levels in the management of the company: functional, divisional, and corporate.

Functional and Operating Causes of the Accident

There were a number of unsafe conditions both on board the ship and at the terminal that affected the operations at the functional (pumping, loading, and shipping the crude oil) level of the company. Had these unsafe conditions been corrected earlier, they probably would have either prevented the occurrence or ameliorated the severity of the oil spill:

Lack of experience by the 3rd officer.   Mr. Cousins, the 3rd mate, either did not realize the need or have the training to disconnect the automatic steering. The orders he gave to the helmsman were correct. The ship did not respond. It is felt that a more experienced officer would have recognized the need to disconnect the automatic steering, or would have called for emergency steering with the engines when the ship did not respond to the first course correction made with the rudder.

Lack of attention by members of the crew.   Every experienced seaman on board must have known that the tanker was far off course, and headed directly towards a submerged reef. It was a clear night. Visibility was over ten miles. The reef location was known, and marked with a lighted buoy. No one voiced any concern, and the single lookout who was on duty was on the bridge, 1,000 feet back from his proper station at the bow. It is felt that had the lookout been at the bow, or had any seaman on duty been attentive, they would have been able to warn the 3rd officer in time for a much earlier course correction.

Lack of emergency equipment at the shore base.   Two barges to carry the containment booms were specified in the emergency oil spill plan; only one was stationed in Valdez, and it had been damaged in a winter storm 9 weeks before the accident. The proper number of booms for containment of the oil spill were not in stock. The proper lengths of hose for transfer of the remaining oil were not available. The emergency lighting system, to help in laying booms and recovering oil at night, could not be found (it had been loaned to a winter carnival). Ten skimmers were available as promised in the plan, but repair parts were not kept in stock, and equipment breakdowns were common as the skimmers were not designed to collect the emulsified "mousse" mixture of oil and water that had formed through wave action in the non-contained spill. Only 69 gallons of chemical dispersants, to break up the mousse into small droplets which would be much easier to collect with the skimmers, were in the warehouse at Valdez and 10,000 gallons were needed to treat an oil spill of this size.

Lack of trained personnel at the shore base.   Prior to 1981 there had been a dedicated oil spill response team of 12 persons stationed at Valdez. This team had been disbanded, as an unnecessary expense, and its duties assigned to the regular employees at the terminal. There had, however, been little training of the regular employees, and consequently there was delay in loading the long and heavy containment booms on the one remaining barge at the terminal, and there was confusion in unloading, connecting, and positioning these booms at the wreck site.

One senior employee said that there had been "zero oil spill training, none" in the years preceding the accident. He said that he had been summoned to a small spill previously, and, "I didn't know what the hell

I was supposed to do, and when I found the guy I was supposed to report to, he did not know what the hell we were supposed to do either. We just stood there watching."[3]

Divisional and Budgetary Causes of the Accident

The Exxon Shipping Company is a wholly-owned division of Exxon U.S.A., which in turn is one of the five regional companies in the Exxon Corporation. Exxon Shipping is responsible for the operations of all company-owned or company-chartered oil tankers in North America, including the Exxon Valdez. The Alyeska Pipeline Service Company is not a wholly-owned division of Exxon; instead, it is a consortium, owned jointly by the seven oil companies that have drilling rights on the North Slope of Alaska, near Prudhoe Bay. As explained previously, Alyeska is responsible for the operation of the oil pipeline from Prudhoe Bay to Valdez and for the management of the oil terminal at Valdez. These were the two divisions that were responsible for the management of the pumping, loading, and shipping operations. There were a number of conditions that existed at both divisions which contributed to the occurrence and the severity of the oil spill.

Overconfidence by the managers of the two divisions.   Oil had been shipped for 18 years through the pipeline and terminal managed by Alyeska, and on the tankers owned or chartered by Exxon Shipping, without a major spill. Apparently, a general feeling that "it can't happen here" developed among the managers of both companies. Many of the shipboard requirements for the use of experienced officers licensed for navigation in the sea channels approaching Valdez, or for the assignment of lookouts on the bow rather than the bridge, had gradually become neglected over the years. Many of the shore terminal requirements for the stocking of equipment and the training of personnel had also become gradually ignored over the years. It is probably fair to say that the wreck of the Exxon Valdez was an accident waiting to happen.

Lack of funding for the managers of the two divisions.   It is probably also fair to say that the managers of the Exxon Shipping Company and the Alyeska Pipeline Service Corporation were not uncaring, uncommitted people who calmly accepted the inevitability of an "accident waiting to happen" in Prince William Sound. They were unable to take precautions against that accident because they managed the pumping, loading, and shipping operations under an ongoing shortage of funds and a continual pressure for profits.

Capital allocations for the purchase of new equipment had often been rejected or delayed. At the time of the accident, a new barge to carry and lay the containment booms—the barge had to have a special hydraulic crane that would adjust to the roughness of the sea in order to properly position the containment booms—had been ordered and built, but it was still in Seattle because the funds to pay for it had been appropriated too late for shipment before the winter storms.

Operating budgets for the expenses of both the ships and the terminal had continually been reduced. Exxon tankers had originally sailed with a crew of 45. This crew size had been gradually reduced to 22 officers and men over the past five years. The company said that new technologies automated the operation of the large tankers, and reduced the need for a larger crew. Crew members said that they were forced to work 15 hours per day while at sea, and that they were exhausted and frequently not alert. As a result, it was said, they often took the easier stations, on the bridge and not on the bow, with the permission of the officers who recognized the symptoms of overwork. It is even claimed that Captain Hazelwood left the bridge and returned to his cabin, not because he had been drinking and was tired, but because there was paperwork that had to be done soon after leaving port, and the ship no longer carried a stenographer/clerk who could prepare those reports.

The same large reductions in staff had occurred at the oil terminal. It has already been explained that the dedicated oil spill response team ("dedicated" meant that the 12 members of that team had no other duties than to be prepared to quickly contain and then recover oil spills in the harbor and sea lanes approaching Valdez) had been disbanded in 1981. The terminal workforce generally had been reduced by 50% from 1986 to 1989, and personnel able to operate the cranes, barges, and tugs were no longer automatically included on every shift. "There was an overall attitude of petty cheapness that severely affected our ability to operate safely" was the statement of a prior manager of the marine operations at the terminal. "I was shocked at the shabbiness of the operations."[4]

Newspaper accounts following the accident supported the allegations of budget shortfalls and insufficient funding. *The Wall Street Journal* reported that one year "Alyeska managers prepared what they thought was a lean budget and presented it to a meeting of the owner's committee (representatives from the seven major oil companies that jointly owned the consortium) in San Francisco. According to former Alyeska officials who were briefed on the meeting at the time, committee members cited a figure, roughly $220 million, and asked if the budget was under that; told that it wasn't, they rejected the proposed budget out of hand."[5]

Corporate and Strategic Causes of the Accident

I think that it is safe to say that the delays in the capital appropriations and the reductions in the expense budgets were not the result of arbitrary decisions by corporate executives and thoughtless procedures by corporate staff. Instead, they were the result of major changes in the corporate strategy, structure, systems, and style which in turn were reactions to major alterations in the economic conditions of the worldwide petroleum industry.

The overriding economic condition in the oil industry during the period 1981 to 1989 was the instability in the price of crude oil. Following the shortages of the Arabian Oil Embargo of 1978 and the Iranian Oil Blockade of 1981, the price of crude oil had risen to $32.00 per barrel, and it was expected to go higher in the years following 1981. Instead, there was an unexpected under-usage by Western Europe, the United States and Japan, an unanticipated overproduction by O.P.E.C. members, and the price of crude oil declined to a low of $12.00 per barrel in 1986. It had only partially recovered to $18.00 per barrel by 1989. Companies such as the Exxon Corporation which produced much of their own crude oil, rather than purchasing that raw material on the open market, had to adjust to much lower profit margins, and they did this by changing the strategy, the structure, the systems, and the style of the firm:

Changes in the corporate strategy. Exxon deliberately attempted to achieve a low cost position in the transportation, refining, and distribution of oil products. Senior executives realized that they could not compete with O.P.E.C. in the low cost production of crude oil, and consequently they "restructured" to reduce the "downstream" expenses. 45,000 employees (out of a total of 145,000) were offered early retirement, and the older, specialized managers and workers who did not accept that offer were forced to resign. No dedicated teams for emergencies such as refinery fires or tanker spills were left in place. No excess staffing for terminals or ships was permitted.

Changes in the organizational structure. Exxon deliberately "flattened" the structure, with fewer layers between senior managers at the corporate level and operating personnel at the functional level. The fewer layers meant reduced supervision of the divisions by the corporate staff, and reduced supervision of operations by the divisional personnel. No longer was an Exxon manager assigned solely to supervise company interests in the Alyeska Pipeline Service Company. Instead, supervision of Alyeska was just one of the responsibilities of the West Coast manager for Exxon U.S.A. Fewer divisional managers were sent to Valdez, and those that were assigned to the oil terminal were responsible for a much wider range of operations. Exxon Shipping suffered from the same reductions in divisional personnel and the same widening of individual responsibilities.

Changes in the managerial systems.   The managerial systems for planning, control, and motivation are interrelated within a company, both conceptually and pragmatically. Strategic planning looks at environmental assumptions, organizational resources, industry economics, and managerial intentions, and then settles upon a long term strategy, or method of competition within the industry. Program planning allocates the resources necessary to implement that strategy. Budgetary planning forecasts the revenues and expenses, and establishes numerical measures of the achievement of the strategy. Operational accounting records the actual results of the achievement in numerical terms, and then comparative evaluation analyzes the variances between the planned outcomes and the actual results.

The comparison between planned outcomes and actual results is the basic control system, or evaluation method, that is in use in nearly every major company worldwide. The control system or evaluation method is almost inevitably connected to the motivation system. Performance that meets or exceeds planned outcomes is rewarded, by bonuses or by promotions. There is, in well managed companies, a direct interrelationship between planning, control, and motivation; these interrelationships can be seen graphically in Exhibit 6–2.

Exxon at the time of the accident in Prince William Sound was a "well managed company." As the strategy and structure of the company shifted, there was a deliberate change in the systems for planning, control, and motivation systems. Planning at the budgetary level began, as has been described, to emphasize cost reductions rather than revenue expansions. Control, which is the comparison of the actual results of operations to the planned outcomes of the budget, also focused on cost reductions. Motivation, which is the award of incentives to the managers whose actual results meet or exceed their planned outcomes, followed in precisely the same pattern.

It was not just that bonuses and promotions tended to follow successful cost reductions in the operations of the pipeline, terminal, and tankers. Executives began to feel that their careers were increasingly at risk due to the forceful downsizing of the firm. One Exxon manager was quoted as saying, "I feel my neck is in the noose. If I don't deliver, they'll get someone in here that will."[6] An Alyeska manager said he was told, "If you can't ship our oil and meet your budget, we'll find somebody else who can."[7]

Changes in the leadership style.   Exxon for years had prided itself on a generous, almost paternalistic attitude towards its employees. Mr. Clifford Garvin, the Chairman of Exxon for nine years prior to the severe downsizing initiated in 1986, had said, "Exxon hasn't existed 104 years without having developed a lot of strengths. No. 1 is the people who are in this company. We have more than our fair share of good people."[8]

EXHIBIT 6–2

Relationship of Planning, Control, and Motivational Systems
in Corporate Management

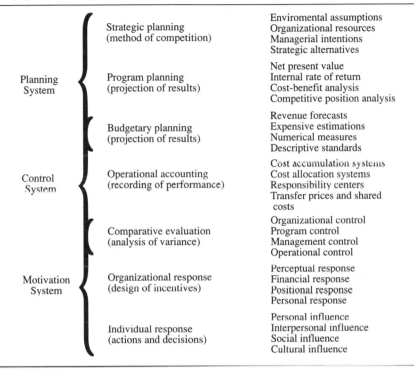

| Planning System | Strategic planning (method of competition) | Enviromental assumptions / Organizational resources / Managerial intentions / Strategic alternatives |

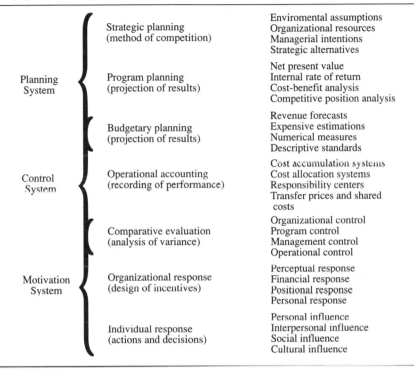

SOURCE: LaRue Hosmer, *Strategic Management: Text and Cases on Business Policy* (Englewood Cliffs, N.J.. Prentice-Hall, 1982), p. 566.

Mr. Lawrence Rawls, who became chairman in 1986 and did initiate the severe downsizing, had a changed attitude towards employees and a different leadership style. "I'm bottom line oriented. I look at the revenues, and then I look at everything that comes in between (that is, the variable costs and fixed expenses). When I find something that looks a little bit soft, I take a *hard* look. When the good times are rolling, you can ignore some of that stuff. But, when times get difficult, you've got to do something. In fact, you should do it anyway. That's management. That's what shareholders pay us for."[9]

Assume that you were a manager assigned to the Alyeska Pipeline Service Company, in charge of inventory control and storage. You know that there are not enough containment booms in stock to handle a large oil spill. You know that there should be two barges on hand but only one is in the harbor, and that one was damaged in a storm 9 weeks previously. You can arrange for replacement of the booms or repair of the barge, but either action will take you far over your budget for the year. You know what has happened to other managers for Exxon who went far over their budgets for the year. You are concerned about a possible oil spill, and the damaging impact that would have upon the environment, but you are also worried about your career. Do you take action? In retrospect, replacement of the booms, hoses, and dispersants and repair of the barge would have been the "right" thing to do. But, do you do the right thing?

Or, assume that you are a manager working for Exxon Shipping. You know that the tankers now carry only two officers (the captain and the 1st mate) who are experienced enough to be licensed to navigate in the sea lanes approaching the port of Valdez. You know that if one of the tankers happens to leave port late at night, an inexperienced officer will be on the bridge for it is traditional for the 3rd mate to take the 12:00 midnight to 4:00 A.M. watch, and for the 2nd mate to take the 4:00 A.M. to 8:00 A.M. duty. You also know that it would be much more expensive to hire experienced officers for those positions. You have the authority to make that decision, but do you? Or, do you say to yourself, "There hasn't been a major oil spill in Prince William Sound for the past 18 years, and, with any luck, there won't be one for the next three to four years while I am responsible for the staffing of the tankers"?

I think that we can agree that the organizational pressures at Exxon— the strategy, the structure, the systems, and the style—all tended to push managers towards saving money by reducing the number of experienced officers on board the tankers, and towards avoiding the capital appropriations and budget expansions necessary to maintain a high state of preparedness at the shore stations. In short, the organizational pressures tended to push managerial decisions and actions strongly towards the economic performance of the firm, and definitely away from the social performance of the company.

What could have been done, at Exxon, to avoid placing managers in this fundamental moral quandary where they had to choose between the economic and social performance of the company, between their careers and their responsibilities? Let us start our investigation of this question by assuming that it was not the intent of Lawrence Rawls, Chairman of the Exxon Corporation and initiator of the downsizing strategy, to reduce costs at the expense of worker protection (refinery fires) or environmental deterioration (tanker spills). Let us assume that he believed that company managers at the divisional and functional levels would know that it was necessary to maintain safe operating conditions despite the strategy that emphasized cost reduction and capital conservation, and despite the control and motivation systems that both measured and rewarded performance based upon those two dimensions.

Given Mr. Rawls' intention of maintaining safe operating conditions despite the cost reduction and capital conservation goals, how could he have conveyed that expectation to all Exxon employees? He could have simply called a series of meetings and talked to the employees. But, there were more than 100,000 employees left even after the restructuring was completed, and these people were spread over the entire globe for Exxon truly was and is an international firm. The meetings would have to be large, to fit in all of the employees in a reasonable time frame, and large meetings offer no opportunity for questions to be answered and illustrations to be given. He could have simply written a series of letters, stressing the need to maintain safe operating conditions. But, mass-mailed letters tend not to be read with great care, and an attempt in one or two pages to explain the desired choice between severe cost reductions and safe operating conditions might have confused more than informed the employees.

Mr. Rawls could, as an alternative to large meetings or mass mailings, have 1) prepared a written code of ethics to convey his expectations on social vs economic performance, have 2) instituted an informal review process to advise on social vs economic performance, or have 3) re-examined the strategy, structure, systems, and style of the company to set clear priorities between social and economic performance. Let us look more closely at each of these three alternatives.

WRITTEN CODE OF ETHICS TO CONVEY PERFORMANCE EXPECTATIONS

A written code of ethics is a statement of the norms and beliefs of an organization. It is an attempt to describe "the way we are going to do things around here," with a particular emphasis upon "actions that are simply not acceptable in this organization." A written code of ethics, in brief, is an attempt to set the moral standards of the firm.

The norms and beliefs in a written code of ethics are generally proposed, discussed, and defined by the senior executives in the firm, and then published and distributed to all of its employees. Norms, of course, are standards of behavior; they are the ways the senior people in the organization want the others to act when confronted with a given situation. An example of a norm in a code of ethics would be, "Employees of this company will not accept personal gifts with a monetary value over $25.00 in total from any business friend or associate, and they are expected to pay their full share of the costs for meals or other entertainment (concerts, the theater, sporting events, etc.) that have a value above $25 per person." The norms in an ethical code are generally expressed as a series of negative statements, for it is easier to list the things a person should not do than to be precise about the things a person should do.

The beliefs in an ethical code are standards of thought; they are the ways that the senior people in the organization want others to think when confronted with a given situation. This is not censorship. Instead, the intent is to encourage ways of thinking and patterns of thought that will lead towards the desired behavior. Consequently, the beliefs in an ethical code are generally expressed in a positive form. "Our first responsibility is to our customers" is an example of a positive belief that sometimes appears in codes of ethics; another would be "We wish to be good citizens of every community in which we operate."

Do ethical codes work? Are they helpful in conveying the moral standards selected by the Board of Directors and president to all others working within the firm? Yes, *provided* those moral standards obviously apply to everyone, not just the personnel at the operating level, *and provided* the Board of Directors and president make an effort to address the moral problems actually faced by employees at the divisional and operating levels.

Many written codes of ethics are just detailed explanations of corporate expectations relative to financial honesty and legal scrupulousness. Look at the summary statements in the code of ethics of Exxon U.S.A., the regional portion of Exxon Corporation responsible directly for Exxon Shipping Company and indirectly for Alyeska Pipeline Service Company. The statements in Exhibit 6–3 can be further summarized as "be honest, be truthful, obey the law, and avoid conflicts of interest." There is certainly nothing wrong with honesty, truthfulness, legality, and the avoidance of conflicts of interest, but I assume that many readers are at least mildly troubled by the apparent direction of the statements at the lower levels of the firm (there is a list of actions that can't be undertaken except with the prior approval "of management"; who approves equivalent actions by those managers?), and by the obvious exclusion from the statements of any expressed concern for worker safety, environmental pollution, customer service, or distributor loyalty.

EXHIBIT 6–3
Summary Code Ethics of Exxon Company, U.S.A.

Business Ethics

Our company policy is one of strict observance of all laws applicable to its business.

A reputation for scrupulous dealing is itself a priceless Company asset.

We do care how we get results.

We expect candor at all levels and compliance with accounting rules and controls.

Antitrust

It is the established policy of the Company to conduct its business in compliance with all state and federal antitrust laws.

Individual employees are responsible for seeing that they comply with the law.

Employees must avoid even the appearance of violation.

Conflict of Interest

Competing or conducting business with the Company is not permitted, except with the knowledge and consent of management.

Accepting and providing gifts, entertainment, and services must comply with specific requirements.

An employee may not use Company personnel, information, or other assets for personal benefit.

Participating in certain outside activities requires the prior approval of management.

SOURCE: Exxon Company, U.S.A. Company document, December 1988.

Now, look at Exhibit 6–4, the written code of ethics of Johnson & Johnson, the large drug company and distributor of medical supplies. There is no mention of financial honesty or legal adherence. Perhaps those virtues are assumed. Instead there is an explicit listing, in an obvious order of priority, of the accepted social responsibilities of the firm. You are certainly welcome to disagree, but I would like to say that I think that the Credo of Johnson & Johnson is an impressive document.

Do they mean it? Are the senior executives at Johnson & Johnson actually willing to place the welfare of their customers, employees, and communities above the profits of their stockholders? Apparently they are, or at least apparently they were at the time of the Tylenol scare in 1982. The company spent over $100 million removing Tylenol (a non-prescription drug that was found to have been deliberately poisoned in Chicago, causing the deaths of four individuals) from the shelves of every

---

EXHIBIT 6–4

Code of Ethics of Johnson & Johnson, Inc.

Our Credo

We believe our first responsibilty is to the doctors, nurses, and patients, to mothers and all others who use our products and services.

In meeting their needs everything we do must be of high quality.

We must constantly strive to reduce our costs in order to maintain reasonable prices.

Customers' orders must be serviced promptly and accurately.

Our suppliers and distributors must have an opportunity to make a fair profit.

We are responsible to our employees, the men and women who work with us throughout the world.

Everyone must respect their dignity and recognize their merit.

We must respect their dignity and recognize their merit.

They must have a sense of security in their jobs.

Compensation must be fair and adequate, and working conditions clean, orderly and safe.

Employees must feel free to make suggestions and complaints.

There must be equal opportunity for employment, development and advancement for those qualified.

We must provide competent management, and their actions must be just and ethical.

We are responsible to the communities in which we live and work and to the world community as well.

We must be good citizens—support good works and charities and bear our fair share of taxes.

We must encourage civic improvements and better health and education.

We must maintain in good order the property we are privileged to use, protecting the enviroment and natural resources.

Our final responsibility is to our stockholders.

Business must make a sound profit.

We must experiment with new ideas.

Research must be carried on, innovative programs developed and mistakes paid for.

New equipment must be purchased, new facilities provided and new products launched.

Reserves must be created to provide for adverse times.

When we operate according to these principles, the stockholders should realize a fair return.

SOURCE: Johnson & Johnson, Inc. Company annual report for 1982, p. 5.

store within the United States. Mr. James Burke, Chairman of Johnson & Johnson, credits the written code of ethics with guiding the actions of his company. "This document spells out our responsibilities to all of our constituencies: consumers, employees, community, and stockholders. It served to guide all of us during the crisis, when hard decisions had to be made in what were often excruciatingly brief periods of time. All of our employees worldwide were able to watch the process of the Tylenol withdrawal and the subsequent reintroduction in tamper-resistant packaging, confident of the way in which the decisions would be made. There was a great sense of shared pride in the knowledge that the Credo was being tested . . . and it worked!"[10]

It is difficult to state the norms and beliefs of an organization relative to the various constituent groups—employees, customers, suppliers, distributors, stockholders, and the general public—clearly and explicitly. Most companies cannot do this in a written code of ethics because they have not thought through, as part of their strategy, structure, and systems, exactly what are those norms and beliefs. I think that we can conclude that written codes of ethics can be effective in guiding the decisions and actions of managers at the divisional and functions levels *provided* the statements clearly reflect the expectations of the senior executives relative to the social performance of the firm in an orderly, prioritized listing, *and provided* it is accepted that those expectations relative to social performance will be maintained despite an adverse impact upon the financial performance of the firm.

INFORMAL REVIEW PROCESS TO ADVISE ON PERFORMANCE EXPECTATIONS

Some companies have set up an informal review process to counsel managers at the divisional and operating levels on ethical problems which involve a conflict between the economic and social performance of the firm. The feeling is that executives in the formal review process, that is executives at a higher level in the structural hierarchy of the firm, are subject to the same organizational pressures as are their subordinates, and consequently are unable to properly advise subordinates. Think for a minute about being the head of the Exxon Shipping Company, given the corporate emphasis upon cost reductions. Would you really want one of your subordinates asking you what to do about the use of inexperienced officers directing oil tankers in and out of the port of Valdez? This is not a very generous view of the process of management, but it is said that many divisional managers in large companies would prefer not to know what can go wrong within their divisions. If you don't know, the reasoning is, you can't really be blamed when something does go wrong. If you do know, then you probably will have to take some action, and that action may not be very popular with the senior executives at the corporate level. It is easy for you to convey to your own subordinates the attitude that you don't want to be bothered with "operating" details; they will have to settle such issues following their own initiative.

As another example, think for a minute about being the head of the Alyeska Pipeline Service Company. Would you really want your subordinates asking you what to do about the shortages of emergency supplies and trained personnel? Again, you might be tempted to tell them that the details of inventory levels and training schedules are their concerns, not yours. You might be worried that your own career would be at risk if you tried to push through the capital appropriations and budget increases necessary to remedy those shortages.

An informal review process provides an indirect, nonthreatening means of obtaining a response from senior management on a conflict between economic and social performance. An ombudsman is appointed. This is a person within an organization, often an older and respected manager, close to retirement, who has been relieved of operating responsibilities and assigned the task of counseling younger employees on career issues, organizational difficulties, and moral problems. The term is Swedish; it originally referred to a government agent in that country who had been especially appointed to investigate complaints made by individual citizens against public officials for abuses of power or unfeeling/uncaring acts. Often the ombudsman, whether in a business firm or public office, can go considerably beyond counseling and investigation, and is able to act informally to resolve moral problems. As an example, we can consider the case of the recent graduate mentioned in the first chapter who was concerned about the inclusion of family vacation tours, country club fees, and sporting event tickets on the expense accounts of many senior executives within her firm. Were there an ombudsman in that company, the recent graduate of a business school who reported the practice to me, could have reported it to the ombudsman. That person could then have counseled the recent graduate to either, "Forget it; that's just part of the accepted pay structure for senior people around here," or (and let us hope this would have been the reaction) the ombudsman could have told her, "You do not need to be concerned any longer; I will take care of the matter, and see that this is stopped, without implicating you in any way." Then, he could have met informally with the president and members of the board of directors, and asked for a clarification of the relevant policy. An older and respected member of a firm, close to retirement yet also close to the president and members of the board, can correct many improper situations informally, without concern for latter retribution.

Does the informal review process symbolized by the ombudsman really work? Again, yes, but only if the person occupying that position is truly clear in his/her own mind on the priorities of the senior executives of the firm. The priorities of the senior executives on questions of economic versus social performance are the true values of the firm. As with written codes of ethics, many times these values have never been explicitly stated or, even better, obviously followed by the senior executives. The ombudsman can help in bringing moral problems to their attention and in asking for clarification, but the person holding that position cannot, by himself or herself, resolve those conflicts between economic and social performance.

RE-EXAMINATION OF THE STRATEGY, STRUCTURE, SYSTEMS, AND STYLE

Written codes of ethics and informal review processes are seldom as effective as might be desired in resolving the conflicts that exist within most companies between the economic and the social performance of the firm. The priorities between economic and social performance are the true values of the firm, but most companies have not thought through, as part of their strategy, structure, systems, and style, exactly what are those values.

It is the argument of this book that senior executives have a responsibility to "think through" the priorities of the firm relative to the conflict between economic and social performance, rather than pushing decisions on those conflicts down to the lower portions of the organization. It is the argument of this book that senior executives have a responsibility to "set" the values of the firm, clearly, for employees at the functional and divisional levels so that they know exactly what is expected of them when they encounter moral dilemmas.

How do senior managers think through these conflicts and set those values? It is suggested that they start with strategic planning, and recognize the effect of alternative strategies upon each of the constituent groups within the organization. "We can increase profits substantially by eliminating the dedicated teams for refinery fires and oil spills at each of our facilities, but what will be the impact of that staffing change upon the safety of our employees and the quality of our environment?" It should have been reasonably clear at the time that the cost reduction strategy was first being considered that such a staffing change could have a very adverse impact upon employee safety and environmental quality, even given the low probability of accidents derived from past data. After all, accidents do happen, and the company should, as part of the strategic planning process, have prepared for the eventuality of an accident. "We recognize that the elimination of the dedicated teams could have an adverse impact upon worker safety and environmental quality, and consequently we will provide meaningful response training for all of our personnel and we will maintain complete emergency supplies at all of our facilities."

Then it is necessary for senior executives, as part of program planning (for resource allocations) and budgetary planning (for revenue and expense projections), to ensure that capital is provided for the emergency supplies and expenses are included for the response training. Next, the control system has to be changed to reflect the altered priorities. It is not enough to simply ask the manager of the oil terminal at Valdez, "Did you meet our revenue and expense projections?" As part of that person's annual review it is necessary to add a number of additional questions. "Is our stock of the emergency supplies needed to contain a major oil spill complete?" "Are the two barges listed in our emergency plan fully maintained and ready for service?" "Are our employees thoroughly trained to respond to a major oil spill, and what was the response time at the most recent training exercise?" Lastly, the motivation system has to be changed, to reflect the different controls. If a bonus is to be paid for keeping within revenue and expense projections, then a bonus should also be paid for maintaining the essential supplies, repairing the emergency equipment, and meeting the response times needed to mitigate an environmental disaster. If that second bonus is not included in the motivation system, it sends a message throughout the organization that the mitigation of environmental disasters is not nearly so important as the improvement of corporate profits.

Thinking through the obligations of the firm towards its different constituencies of customers, employees, owners, etc., and setting the values of the firm on its various conflicts between economic and social outcomes are not easy tasks. It is hard to recognize all the obligations and anticipate all the conflicts, but it is even more difficult to know exactly what to do about them. We saw in the last chapter, on the ethical choice of individuals, that there are no completely satisfactory means of reaching a decision when confronted by a moral dilemma. We have to conclude in this chapter, on the ethical design of organizations, there are no completely satisfactory means of setting a strategy when confronted with obligations to different groups and conflicts between different outcomes. Multiple analysis—using economic, legal, and moral forms of reasoning—does appear to clarify the issues, and does seem to generate solutions that can be considered to be more "right," more "just," and more "fair" than solutions that do not make use of the multiple forms of analysis, but that process of analysis does not guarantee either unanimity or certainty. It does not guarantee unanimity because the values—the priorities between economic, legal, and moral outcomes—are bound to differ between members of the organization. It does not guarantee certainty because the probabilities—the chances of those outcomes actually occurring—are bound to be unknown.

What were the probabilities of the Exxon Valdez actually running aground on Bligh Reef, 10 miles south of her proper course through Prince William Sound? Prior to the accident, those probabilities could not have been calculated. Could the senior management at Exxon have agreed upon the "proper" level of preparation for that potential accident? Probably not. Yet, business firms have to be managed with the recognition that they do have obligations to a wide range of constituencies and that they will encounter conflicts between economic and social outcomes. How can this be done?

THE MORAL RESPONSIBILITIES
OF SENIOR MANAGEMENT

In most companies under current conditions the obligations to different constituencies and the conflicts between different outcomes are simply ignored by senior management. The attitude generally is that those obligations and conflicts are "operating problems"—after all, they deal with such issues as hiring experienced versus inexperienced 2nd and 3rd officers for the tankers, or scheduling crane operators for all shifts at the terminals—and they are pushed down to the divisional and functional levels. The problem is that at those levels most conflicts between economic and social outcomes will be settled in favor of the economic side of the balance. Why? Because under existing managerial systems, the performance of those managers is measured by economic criteria and their future is dependent upon economic results.

The obligations to the different constituencies and the conflicts between the different outcomes have to be addressed and resolved at the senior level, as part of the strategic planning process? Senior managers have to recognize the potential impacts of the alternative strategies upon the different constituencies of the firm. Senior managers have to anticipate the potential conflicts within the alternative strategies of the economic and social performance levels of the firm. And they have to decide, and then convey that decision to others.

How can this be done, given the lack of certainty and the lack of unanimity that are inherent in the strategic planning process? My response is with character and courage. This is the character to face the obligations and conflicts—not to sidestep or avoid them—and the courage to thoughtfully evaluate each of the alternatives, and then arrive at a solution. This is the character to recognize moral problems, and the courage to express ethical decisions.

Others may disagree with the ethical decision of an executive because of differences in their perspectives within the firm, or because of differences in their beliefs in the importance of the economic outcomes, the legal requirements, the moral principles of benevolence and consistency, or the moral values of justice and liberty. We have a multitude of economic, legal, and ethical outcomes, requirements, principles, and values, but no clear ordering between them. This is not an excuse, however to avoid making ethical decisions in management. We have to make those decisions based upon our sense of responsibility to others; it is a test of our character and a measure of our courage.

Footnotes

1. *The Wall Street Journal,* March 31, 1989, p. 1.
2. Ibid.
3. *The Wall Street Journal,* July 6, 1989, p. 1.
4. Ibid.
5. Ibid.
6. *Business Week,* July 15, 1988, p. 107.
7. Statement of oil industry executive, made in confidence to the author.
8. *Fortune,* January 6, 1986, p. 20.
9. *Fortune,* April 14, 1986, p. 27.
10. Annual Report of Johnson & Johnson, 1982, p. 2.

CASE 6-1

Three Companies in Need of Moral Direction

Three short cases were published earlier in the book that depicted moral problems encountered by recent graduates of a program in business administration. These cases—"Sarah Goodwin," "Susan Shapiro," and "George Kacmarek"—depicted very fundamental moral problems for in each instance they placed the career of the individual in jeopardy if he or she refused to accept the situation. The recent graduates had to decide what they would or would not accept, that is, they had to decide where they would "draw the line."

Now, you have been promoted. Put yourself in the place of the president of one of those companies. Just to help your memory, the moral problems involved 1) a retail store that was shipping defective food products to the ghetto for sale to the poor; 2) a chemical company that maintained a production process even though it was harmful to the health and well-being of the employees; and 3) a plant manager for a metal stamping company who was accepting kickbacks from a steel supplier.

You are the president or a senior vice president, clearly at a managerial level where you can make whatever decision you believe would serve the best interests of your company and your society. You also have a reputation as a "doer," a man or woman who has managed the company very successfully in the past, with continually rising sales and profits, and consequently a person who tends to get his or her own way in dealing with stockholders, board members, and immediate subordinates. In short, no one will openly oppose you. That does not mean, however, that people further down in the organization, at the functional or operating levels, will automatically accept your directions just because they are your directions. You probably will have to convince people that it is in their best interests to follow your directions.

Lastly, you have just found that the situation described in the case actually exists in your firm and, even worse, you have hard evidence that it is endemic throughout the firm. That is, if you decided to be president of the metal stamping company, you have irrefutable evidence that numerous people throughout the company are accepting small kickbacks. If, instead, you put yourself in the place of the president of the chemical company, you now understand that almost all of your chemical plants have at least one production process that is technically legal but medically and environmentally harmful. You are shocked. You say to your spouse that night, "I had no idea this was going on, but it obviously is and I've got to do something about it."

Class Assignment.   What exactly will you do? You can fire the people involved, but will that really cure the problem? What actions can you take that will "cure the problem"?

CASE 6–2

What Do You Do Now?

Frequently as a manager you will find that your views as to what is "right" and "just" and "proper" are not as widely shared as you might have thought. Then you are either forced to take some action, or to ignore the situation. What would you do in each of these instances:

1. *You are the senior vice president of a machinery manufacturing firm* that builds and sells equipment for complete chemical processes on a worldwide basis. The design of this equipment is highly technical, and almost all of your younger employees have an engineering background. Perhaps 15% of those engineers are women, who started joining the company about 5 years previously. It is accepted that the career path for younger employees has to include an overseas assignment in developing countries, and you plan to appoint a woman to the next available opportunity. The vice president of the South American sales division calls you— evidently anticipating your intention—and asks you not to do so. He says that the firm's clients in those Latin countries will not accept women in a technical capacity. "The older men will be polite to her, and treat her like a daughter. The younger ones will engage in some harmless flirting which I assume she can handle with ease, and some not so harmless which she will have to learn to live with. But, neither the older nor the younger customers will accept technical recommendations from a woman, so that she will be useless in a sales capacity. If she wants to work in design at our central office and have no contact with clients, that's fine, but otherwise I think you should send her to Europe." Company sales in Europe were minimal, due to strong competition from technically advanced German, French, and Italian firms.

2. *You are the chief financial officer of a chain of retail stores.* One of your most valued employees came to your department when your company acquired a much smaller chain for which he worked. Most of the staff employees of that chain were discharged as part of a cost reduction program at the time of the acquisition, but you kept this person because his background was very good—his resume showed that he was the graduate of a well known Eastern business school—and because he was obviously very bright and competent. He had been promoted a number of times since then, and now worked regularly as your assistant. You have been asked to give a talk to the students at the well known Eastern business school. After that talk, at lunch, you mention to the Director of Placement how pleased you are with the work of your assistant, and you give his name (which happens to be unusual and memorable) and say that he graduated six years previously. There is an awkward silence. Then the Director of Placement asks, "Are you certain?" He repeats the name and says, "He used to work for me, as my assistant, but if we are talking about the same person I don't believe he is a graduate of this school."

3. *You are the executive vice president of the automotive division* at Sears Roebuck. The automotive division sells tires, batteries, repair parts, and auto accessories, and provides repair/maintenance services, at Sears stores nationwide. You have just learned that the California Department of Consumer Affairs (CDCA) is going to sue Sears Roebuck for customer fraud. The CDCA says that it brought special "test" cars to 48 Sears Auto Centers within the state of California a total of 285 times. The cars were older, but all of the wheel suspension and brake parts—with the exception of the brake pads themselves—had either been recently replaced or had been certified to be in good working order. The driver of the test car, often a woman, asked to have the brake pads—which were worn—replaced under a Sears' printed advertisement offering a "complete brake job for just $48.00." In 247 of those 285 test cases the customer was told that the brake calipers, shock absorbers, coil springs, idler arms, or master cylinders also needed to be replaced at a much higher price. In some instances the undercover investigators were charged as much as $500 for needless repairs. The CDCA claimed that the "customer service representatives" in the auto service areas of Sears stores were paid an escalating commission for the higher value parts, and also were evaluated by a control system that specified the number of these higher value parts that should be sold during every eight hour shift. Customer sales reps who did not meet those sales targets were demoted to the position of regular sales clerks. You had designed both the incentive system and the control system about three years previously, and have since received substantial bonuses based upon the expanded sales and profits that came from the introduction of those systems.

Class Assignment.   Describe the actions that you would take as a senior executive at each of these firms.

CASE 6–3

McKinstry Advertising Agency

You are the president of the McKinstry Advertising Agency, a medium sized firm that specializes in preparing the marketing strategies, performing the market research studies, arranging the distribution channels, and designing the advertising and promotional materials for industrial companies that have developed "off-shoot" consumer products. You obviously serve a very specific niche. Your clients are industrial companies—that is, they sell primarily to other manufacturing firms and government agencies—that have developed—as unintended outcomes of their R&D programs—products for the retail trade. Dow Chemical Company, while not a client of your agency, is an almost ideal example of this type of firm. They have developed and currently produce and market such consumer products as Dow Bathroom Cleaner and Ziploc Bags that in total amount to only 5.8% of Dow's total sales.

Your clients tend not to be as large as Dow Chemical Company nor as well established in consumer marketing. Most have had very little experience in retail sales, and they generally are not very sophisticated in advertising methods. They tend, therefore, to rely heavily upon the advice of the account executives and advertising experts at your agency, and to develop relationships with those people that are far more permanent and personal than is common in the "what have you done for me lately" culture of the consumer products advertising industry.

The "permanent and personal" relationships that are typical of your company but not of industry in general seem to be the cause of a major problem that you have recently encountered. One of your larger clients developed a new type of radar detector. Radar detectors, also known as "fuzzbusters," are simple but extremely sensitive radio receivers that are tuned to the wave length of the police radar. When a car equipped with a detector first enters the radar field a warning light flashes or a buzzer sounds enabling the driver to slow down, if necessary, before the speed of the car can be calculated by the police equipment. The use of radar detectors, thus enables drivers to avoid being stopped and fined for speeding.

Speeding is alleged to be responsible for many traffic accidents. There were 27.7 million traffic accidents involving passenger cars in 1990, and 6.1 million traffic accidents involving trucks. These 33.8 million traffic accidents resulted in 46,400 deaths, 1.8 million severe injuries that required hospitalization, 7.8 million moderate injuries that required attention by medical personnel, extensive slight injuries, uncounted personal traumas, and huge financial losses.

Speeding was said to be a factor in 65% of all traffic accidents, and in 87% of those that caused deaths and severe injuries due to the greater impacts that come from the higher speeds, but it has to be admitted that neither statistic is totally reliable. Police estimate speed based upon the length of skid marks and the extent of physical damage, but those estimates obviously are inexact. Further, "speeding" is defined as any vehicle velocity above the posted limit, and it is claimed that the posted limit is considerably below the safe capability of modern cars and highways in many instances.

Vehicle speed, moreover, is only one of the factors that cause traffic accidents. Alcohol intoxication is believed to be associated with 28% of all accidents and 48% of all accidents that result in death and severe injury. Often speed and intoxication together are held to be the cause. Again, though, there is a problem in measuring intoxication. The percentage of alcohol in the bloodstream that impairs physical response time and personal judgment varies with the body weight, physical conditioning, and drinking history of the individual. Police and medical attendants use a test that takes into account only body weight and, further, it is said by representatives of the licensed beverage (that is, beer, wine, and liquor) industry that the legal threshold for intoxication has been set much too low. Most drivers would be considered to be "driving under the influence" if they consumed two to three glasses of beer or wine within 30 minutes of an accident.

In summary, it cannot be said that the exact causes of most severe traffic accidents are known with certainty but it is believed that speeding and drinking, jointly or separately, play some role in the events that lead up to those accidents. Also to blame, in many instances, are the design of the highway, the condition of the weather, the maintenance of the vehicle, the time of the day (many severe accidents occur at dusk, with poor lighting and tired drivers), and the presence of radar detectors. A study by the Ohio State Police found that radar detectors were present in at least one of the vehicles involved in 69% of all severe traffic accidents on the highways of that state in 1990. Studies in other states have confirmed that finding, with some estimates of the relationship running as high as 75%.

The use of radar detectors is illegal in many if not most states, but neither the manufacturing nor the marketing of the units has ever been banned by the federal government which, of course, is the sole authority which could regulate their interstate trade. The U.S. constitution forbids any state from restricting "imports" from any other state. Currently, therefore, there often occurs an unusual situation in which the use of the radar detector sets may be illegal within a given state, but the sale of those sets is not illegal and cannot be prohibited within that state.

The manufacture and marketing of radar detectors was an expanding industry, with total sales revenues reaching $67 million in 1991, until the police in a number of states began to use lasers rather than radars to apprehend speeders. Lasers project focused beams of light waves rather than focused beams of radio waves, and consequently they cannot be "picked up" by most radar detectors.

Your client, as an offshoot of contract research for the defense industry, has developed a new technology that does "pick up" the light waves far enough away from the source so that drivers can slow down. A full explanation of the technology is not needed; it is probably sufficient to say that the device works on the principle that the light waves from a police laser interfere with a certain spectrum of exceedingly short-range radio signals broadcast from the detector set in the owner's car, and that interference can be detected even though the police car is out-of-sight, perhaps 1/4 mile ahead on the highway, and the police laser is not targeted on this particular car. The proposed design also picks up the interference from a police radar device equally well.

The electronics firm that developed the new radar/laser detection came to the account executive at your agency and requested a marketing plan supported by market research. The marketing plan was developed; it had a heavy emphasis upon direct distribution supported by extensive advertising. The market research was completed; it showed that the first entrant into this field with a new technology could rapidly build market share. The client requested that a young associate who had prepared a very successful advertising program for one of their earlier products be assigned to design the promotional materials for this new one.

The associate, Marilynn Schaefer, refused, saying privately that she felt that it was not "right" to market radar and/or laser detectors that led to more numerous and more severe highway accidents and to greater incidents of death, suffering, and injury. The program director proposed other employees at the associate level within the creative segment of the firm, but the client's representative wanted Marilynn Schaefer to do the work. She continued to refuse, though expressing her reasons only to the account executive, George Sarbo. Eventually the conflict between these two people reached the stage at which George said to Marilynn, "Either work on this account for me or don't work at this agency for anyone" and fired her.

Marilynn Schaefer immediately came to you, as president of the agency, saying that it was not right to fire a person because of her moral beliefs. George Sarbo quickly followed, saying that for 20 years he had followed the stated agency policy of providing clients with personalized service, and that if Marilynn did not want to do so she could not work for him and she should not work for the agency. He also said that if Marilynn were retained at the agency he would leave. You realize that George Sarbo is one of only three account executives at your firm, that he has a very loyal following of clients, and that he might well be able to take those clients with him if he indeed did decide to leave.

Further conversations with both of the participants in the dispute and with the industrial client on the following day showed no change in their positions. The client's representative clearly felt that the delay in assigning Ms. Schaefer to work on the needed advertising was due only to the press of other accounts upon her time; he stated that he felt that he was "owed" her assistance on this project.

Class Assignment.   As president of the agency, what do you do?

Index